HACK LEARNING
ANTHOLOGY

Thanks for
helping me
#HackLearning!

HACK LEARNING ANTHOLOGY

Innovative Solutions for Teachers and Leaders

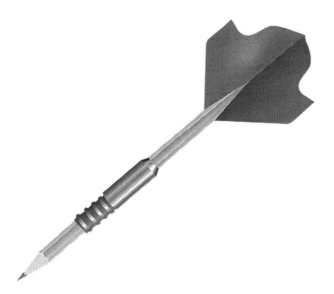

Edited by
Mark Barnes

X10
PUBLICATIONS

These books are available at special discounts when purchased in quantity for use as premiums, promotions, fundraising, and educational use. For inquiries and details, contact us at Times10Books.com

Published by Times 10
Cleveland, OH
Times10Books.com

Cover Design by Tracey Henterly
Interior Design by Steven Plummer
Content Editing by Mark Barnes
Editing by Ruth Arseneault
Proofreading by Jennifer Jas

Library of Congress Control Number: 2017900338

ISBN: 9780986104992

First Printing: February, 2017

TABLE OF CONTENTS

THE HACK LEARNING SERIES

FOREWORD

THE WORD "HACKER" became a favorite part of my vocabulary when I first saw the movie *Jurassic Park*. The boy, Tim, calls Lex, his sister, a computer nerd, and she abruptly replies, "I prefer to be called a hacker." Later, that precocious, self-proclaimed hacker provides some nifty computer coding that ultimately saves everyone from being eaten by diabolical raptors and other ravenous dinosaurs.

Even though they were fictional, her heroics made me an instant fan of Lex, the young hacker in *Jurassic Park*. You see, she didn't steal top-secret government files or surreptitiously empty the bank accounts of hundreds of unsuspecting retirees. Rather, she saw a problem, used the assets she had at her fingertips, and concocted a solution that no one else could see. She didn't need a committee or a five-year plan. Lex, the hacker, had all she needed—a problem, a unique skillset, and a little finesse.

Lex is one of my favorite movie characters because of her courage in the face of incredible odds and because she taught me that hackers are not the dangerous predators they're made out to be. In fact, most hackers have the potential to be heroes.

So, when I decided to write a book about practical solutions for educators, I knew the title long before penning a single word of content. *Hacking Education: 10 Quick Fixes for Every School* was the perfect moniker for a book designed to show people how to attack problems, much as Lex did in *Jurassic Park*. It was the perfect title for a book aimed at inspiring teachers to become hackers.

About a month into writing *Hacking Education*, I suggested a chapter on student-centered learning to my co-author Jennifer Gonzalez, who argued that the topic was too broad for a single chapter. "That might be a whole book," Jennifer said. The more topics we bandied about, the more ideas cropped up for other books. Ultimately, *Hacking Education* became the first book in the Hack Learning Series—books that solve big problems with simple ideas.

The idea of Hack Learning is spreading rapidly and now a book series has morphed into Twitter chats, online courses, keynote speeches, TED talks, podcasts, and online study groups. Educators around the world are integrating various hacks from the books into their classrooms and schools. Hack Learning is now a movement promoting practical, simple, progressive problem-solving, using a hacker's mentality. Lex may be merely a fictional character, but I think she would be proud.

THE ANTHOLOGY

When someone tweeted about the Pineapple Chart being her favorite part of *Hacking Education*, this prompted other readers to regularly tweet their favorite hacks from other books. It struck me one day that there might be enough popular strategies in the Hack Learning Series for an anthology of favorite hacks.

Selecting favorite hacks from each book was no small task (of course, we at Times 10 Books believe every single one is wonderful); fortunately, we had plenty of help. Some were easy decisions, based on the wealth of discussion about them on various social media. The Pineapple Chart, for example, has its own Twitter hashtag and many teachers are sharing it at conferences and with colleagues at neighboring schools. Other strategies, like Vigor Versus Rigor from *Hacking the Common Core*, sparked controversy because they confront trendy words or concepts and ultimately inspire change.

In a few cases, the selection and placement of a "favorite Hack" just felt right. Opening the book with Create C.U.L.T.U.R.E from *Hacking Leadership*, for instance, seems appropriate because so much of Hack Learning is about communicating effectively with all education stakeholders. Ending the book with James Sturtevant's heartfelt conclusion of *Hacking Engagement* is ideal because few people capture the essence and pure joy of teaching like Sturtevant does.

WHAT'S INSIDE?

Forgive the cliché, but it is what it is…sort of. Hack Learning's lead interior designer pulled the selected chapters for the anthology from his archive of previously designed Hack Learning books and inserted them into this book. Thus, each Hack in this book appears exactly as it does in its original book, so each chapter you encounter has a different look and feel than the prior chapter. This is hacky, we think, because it gives someone who has previously read a Hack Learning book a chance to see what other books look like and to try some new strategies, and the educator who has never heard of Hack Learning can take our unique problem-solving formula for a test drive, while enjoying a variety of chapter designs.

INNOVATION

Granted, my opinion may be biased, but I believe Hack Learning brings the kind of innovation that is sorely lacking in education. Our students need innovative teachers and leaders, and our authors provide inventive, practical, often overlooked solutions to many big problems that make innovative teaching and learning easy. There is much more innovation coming in future books.

For now, these are, we believe, Hack Learning's most popular Hacks. Enjoy.

—MARK BARNES, PUBLISHER OF THE HACK LEARNING SERIES

CREATE C.U.L.T.U.R.E.
Start with school leaders

If you get the culture right, most of the other stuff will just happen naturally on its own.
—TONY HSIEH, CEO, ZAPPOS.COM

THE PROBLEM: SCHOOL LEADERS UNDERESTIMATE THEIR IMPACT

ALTHOUGH SCHOOL CULTURE can be defined and described in many ways, every definition ultimately circles back to leadership. A school leader doesn't single-handedly create the school's culture, but that one person does have the greatest impact on the way a school's culture feels. The actions of many—students, staff, families—express and perpetuate that culture, but the tone and leadership style of the school leader thrust the school into a positive or negative trajectory.

One of the tricky aspects of defining a school's culture is that it's not a fixed entity. Culture reflects the feelings and perceptions people experience in a school, which in a healthy environment evolve over time. Many variables cause school culture to transform itself, unless the school's dynamic is stagnant, in which case feelings and perceptions won't evolve. In that case, the culture of a school seems static, fixed. Culture feels so entrenched in tradition that no change seems possible. "Culture" then becomes code for "this is the way we have always done things," and an excuse for not embracing innovation and evolution.

Even this negative school culture can be traced back to the leader of the organization. A staid, arrogant, or incompetent manager will perpetuate a negative culture. A confident, informed, and compassionate instructional lead learner will propagate a positive culture. Creating a positive school culture is a responsibility any school leader must recognize and take seriously.

THE HACK: NURTURE A POSITIVE C.U.L.T.U.R.E.

Any successful hack of a school necessitates developing an understanding of that particular culture, determining how it feels to the educators within the organization. We created the acronym C.U.L.T.U.R.E. to help school leaders with this hack:

Communication
Uncovers
Learning
Transparency
Ultimately
Reveals
Everything

Communication is the beating heart of school culture. The positive impact of an accessible school leader who communicates well and relates well with others circulates throughout the entire system. Clear, consistent communication fosters transparency so all members of the school community share important information. Whether the communication is about curricular decisions that affect teachers or changes in policy that concern students and their families, if leaders communicate in a genuine way, the trust they earn contributes to an even more positive environment. Be aware, though, that constant communication and transparent practice have positive effects only if a school leader can personally validate that his or her decisions have been made to benefit the children.

When the culture values the important work of learners and educators, a school's focus centers exactly where it should. On the learning. School culture cannot be separated from school leaders, because the actions of the individual directly shape and influence the organization's norms.

After amplifying the school's culture and collective vision beyond the walls of your school, pause and ask those around you how that message is resonating with them.

As educator and author, Todd Whitaker, shared in his book *What Great Principals Do Differently*, if the principal sneezes the whole school community catches a cold. As leaders, whether of the school or the classroom, we set the tone for the space. What we value and emphasize eventually permeates the classroom or building. If we focus on mandates, policies, and test scores, then that will set the tone in the building; that will become the culture of the space. Since we have a tremendous impact on the culture, keep it positive and build healthy relationships with all members of the community to reinforce a positive and productive culture.

WHAT YOU CAN DO TOMORROW

The prospect of shaping a school's culture can be overwhelming for a leader because of its abstract nature. Unfortunately, thinking about it will not effect change; instead of being stifled by trepidation, a leader must take action. Since communication can have the greatest impact, that is the perfect place to start hacking school culture.

- **Feed people.** If you have inherited a school where the culture is hard to conceptualize or define, then make time for informal discussions and relationship-building. One of the best ways to facilitate these informal gatherings is to feed people, because being together around food helps people get comfortable; they will linger and information will flow more readily. Whether it means keeping a bowl of candy in your office, getting bagels for breakfast, or ordering pizza for lunch, feed teachers often. Conversation will grow and you will begin to find the pulse of the staff, which is the perfect starting point for building culture.

- **Define the status of your school's culture.** It is surprising how infrequently school leaders talk explicitly about school culture with members of the community. Although it's common to discuss collective vision, non-negotiable priorities, or educational philosophy, it's less usual to initiate dialogue on this significant dynamic. Defining and reflecting on the current status is the best first step to initiating effective change. You can gather information virtually through a survey or personally during a faculty gathering, but it is important that the conversation starts with the staff. Culture begins within the building and spreads beyond it. Pose the following questions to your staff in advance of discussing them in a face-to-face meeting:

  1. *What is the culture of our school?*

  2. *What makes our school different than any other school?*

3. *What feelings and emotions are evoked when you think about our school?*

4. *How can we continue to shape the trajectory of the culture in positive ways?*

- **Share the communication plan with families.** Once you have defined the school's culture with your team, decide how you will communicate it and all the other amazing things happening in your school with your families. Schools can no longer function as fortresses that close out the surrounding community; instead, creating high levels of transparency through a constant flow of communication is critical. Families should have access to relevant and dynamic information. We must harness the power of digital tools to help accelerate and amplify our story beyond the walls of our schools. Pick one platform—maybe Facebook or Twitter or Google Docs—and start sharing the different aspects of your school's C.U.L.T.U.R.E.

- **Name social media interns of the week.** Make visible the wonderful educational opportunities that educators are giving your students and let the kids relay that information. Embrace the possibilities of students telling their stories by implementing a "social media intern" or "tweeter of the week" program in your school. (You might create an "Instagrammer of the week" or "Snapchatter of the week" if Twitter is not your preferred platform.) Classroom teachers could assign students to take on this job for the week to tell their classroom's stories via the social media account. Before turning control over to the students, the teacher could put any necessary parameters in place. For example, "The teacher must approve any post before it goes live." In the primary grades, where the children may not be ready to navigate a social media platform, create the job of "photographer of the week" so the students can capture images that an adult will share on social media posts. Schools have incredible stories and children are some of the best storytellers, so empower them to shape the narrative of your school.

A BLUEPRINT FOR FULL IMPLEMENTATION

Step 1: Build ongoing communication with all stakeholders.

Once you have developed an understanding of school culture, share your findings. Disseminate the message, "This is who we are and this is where we are headed together," in emails, newsletters, video updates, and face-to-face encounters. Make sure that this message features the locations where stakeholders meet: PTA meetings, faculty gatherings, social media. Taking care to be consistent in the way the school gets presented develops a cohesive understanding throughout the community.

Step 2: Educate families and staff.

The reality is that some families have a negative perception about social media, so it is imperative that they are educated about any platforms you are using. For example, if you decide to start with Twitter, hold several Twitter 101 sessions at times that are convenient for both families and staff to attend. Make sure to publicize the sessions in advance so people can save the date. Provide people with information and resources via email and through handouts during the sessions to correct any skewed perceptions they may have about social media. Show them how it works, show them how it will be used, and give them time to set up an account and explore the platform themselves. Finally, consider having someone record your session so it can be shared with anyone who couldn't attend.

Step 3: Ask questions.

After amplifying the school's culture and collective vision beyond the walls of your school, pause and ask those around you how that message is resonating with them. Question members from a cross section of the community to take the "temperature" of how people are responding to the school story. Ask for feedback during informal conversations at the drop off/pick up areas, before or after PTA meetings, while you are passing through the faculty lounge, or via a short survey of no more than three questions that will take five minutes or less to answer. Although informal face-to-face conversations will perhaps give you more information because they allow you to register tone of voice, body language, and eye contact, the survey allows everyone to participate. If the message "sticks" on both personal and professional levels, then you have achieved sustainability. Even once you judge the culture to be sustainable, continue to ask questions, but don't limit it to only once a year—take a reading of the culture at least four or five times a year.

Step 4: Hand the microphone over to the community.

After it is clear that your school culture is in a positive state and everyone is aware of the common vision, empower all members of the community to share the school's stories from their perspectives. For example, every week at Cantiague Elementary, six students from each class research what's happening at each grade level and film their updates to share from the school YouTube channel. Showing what's happening in your school supports and inspires the staff, validates and encourages the students, and informs and enlightens the broader community about the school's C.U.L.T.U.R.E. We make the video updates as easy as possible in two ways: 1) We set up a calendar using Google Docs so teachers know in advance when their classes are up, and 2) We created a list of the steps students need to follow so they know what to anticipate. Typically, after the teachers select students, the group of children meets with the principal on Monday to go over the plan and then reconvenes later in the week to make the video when the children have gathered all the necessary information.

Step 5: Hone the vision.

As you build culture, continue to hone your vision of what that culture might become. Putting out fires and solving problems aren't enough to create an ideal school even when the systems you've put into place are thriving. Even a school with a strong positive culture can work on becoming a better iteration of itself. Enlist your "dream team" of students, teachers, and families to help hone the vision by generating a list of priorities for continued growth and revising the plan according to progress. Stasis leads to entropy in school culture as in nature. Breathe life into your school by keeping the culture vital and by seeking improvement.

OVERCOMING PUSHBACK

Even considering the significant influence an instructional lead learner has on creating a positive school culture, one cannot ignore the influence others have on the organization. Not everyone in the school may be supportive of the school leader's efforts to promote a positive school culture; in fact, some people may be intent on sabotaging it so it becomes divisive, negative, and potentially destructive.

Using social media to amplify school culture puts kids at risk. Social media usage is a hot topic in many schools and districts. Unfortunately, negative associations with social media cause hesitance about engaging with digital platforms. School leaders avoid social media because of concerns about everything from being publicly bashed to exposing students to online predators. Social media sites such as Twitter and Instagram conjure up thoughts of frivolous celebrities sharing minute-by-minute breakdowns of their daily activities, or worse, of well-publicized episodes of cyberbullying. The negative discourse around social media causes leaders to avoid it in many schools despite its obvious benefits.

Demystify the misconceptions that surround social media and consider the powerful opportunities these free resources offer to you as a school leader and to your community. Start by focusing on learning: Educate all members of the community about how the various social media platforms work and how to use them for positive purposes. For example, many schools have offered their staff voluntary training sessions on how to use social media sites. Because they know that knowledge is power, some school leaders have invited families in for Social Media 101 presentations to reframe their perceptions, allay their fears, and answer their questions. Finally, school leaders model appropriate digital citizenship by actively using social media for professional purposes, including developing a PLN for personal and professional development; creating a school hashtag to crowdsource information; and sharing pictures that demonstrate the importance of what happens in school.

Parents don't want their children on our social media stream. After sharing an outline of how you communicate with families using digital tools and social media, give families the opportunity to opt their children out if they are not comfortable having their pictures or stories used. Send a letter home explaining that in addition to the traditional media platforms such as newspapers and television news that might feature stories and pictures connected to the school, you are now integrating tools such as social media to accelerate and amplify the school story. If they don't want their children featured they must communicate that to you in writing. We have found that it is easier to handle families that may want to opt out as opposed to trying to get every family to sign off on a permission slip.

Staff morale is low and people are stressed out, so how can I broach the subject of C.U.L.T.U.R.E. with them? Even where there is a positive school culture, educators are constantly assailed by mandates that create stress and anxiety. Over the last several years we have seen this type of situation repeatedly when changes such as the Common Core Learning Standards or linking educator evaluations and high stakes test scores have made educators feel targeted, attacked, and disrespected. For many this is a daily reality, but that doesn't have to be the case.

Policies and mandates affect all schools, but school leaders determine how they manifest in the classroom and affect the educators. For example, a couple of years ago the New York State Education Department shared standardized instructional modules for English Language Arts on their EngageNY website. The materials weren't mandated by the state, so they didn't necessarily have to work their way into the classroom. Unfortunately, many school leaders took the availability of resources as a mandate and went online, printed out all the materials, created binders for the teachers, handed them out, and told the teachers to begin implementing the "curriculum" A.S.A.P. As one can imagine, this caused the morale in many schools to bottom out and school culture to spiral downward. There was no communication, there was no reflection—misinformed leaders made the decision irrespective of the impact.

This scenario does not have to reflect how we handle mandates and policies in our schools. Instead of lunging to implement policy changes, a transformational instructional lead learner will pause to review a policy's expectations and engage various community members on how it can be most meaningfully integrated into their school.

The keys to success are communication, reflection, and collaborative decision-making. If those techniques are employed, morale will remain high and culture will stay positive.

How can we increase test scores if we're focused on culture?

Culture and test scores don't have to be mutually exclusive. We can definitely focus on school culture and know that in the long term positive culture will have an impact on test scores. For example, we know that when children attend a school where they feel valued, confident, and happy, their brains release endorphins, which benefits their learning. When students are actively engaged in and have ownership of their learning, chances are they will perform well in all academic areas. Of course, this is only possible if the teachers are feeling similarly. To create a setting where students and teachers thrive and feel genuine joy, leaders must focus on school culture. The choice is yours: Get short-term results by investing in disconnected test prep activities, or lay the foundation for long-term results that can be transformational on many levels for years to come by investing in positive school culture.

THE HACK IN ACTION

Creating a vision statement is an integral step in communicating the school's C.U.L.T.U.R.E. But it is not necessarily an easy process that a leader can tackle in isolation.

Tony's Story

Revamping the Cantiague vision statement was something I had been struggling with for years because I wasn't quite sure about the best way to capture and represent our vision so that it clearly communicated the culture of Cantiague Elementary. So, three years ago our shared decision-making team of students, family members, and staff was charged with the important task of rewriting and recreating the school vision statement so it captured the essence of our culture. We wanted to amplify it so it reached far beyond the walls of our school.

We started by listing words that we felt best described Cantiague and the Cantiague experience. Generating that list, which ended up being about a hundred words and phrases, and then narrowing it down was quite a process. It involved surveys of staff, families, and kids; discussions; more surveys; and follow-up discussions. It took us months. After deciding on the words that best fit Cantiague we then shifted the conversation to what our vision statement should actually look like. Will we generate a bulleted list? Maybe we could write it in a different way? Should we go in a completely different direction and create a Wordle that would be permanently visible on our website? Although we engaged in rich discussion, we had a tough time coming to a conclusion.

The team kept coming back to the idea that a video might best capture the Cantiague experience. It would allow us to literally show our school vision using images of the life of the school. Thanks to the hard work of our team, the vision statement went from an idea to a video reality. We communicated what made us Cantiague, we uncovered the learning, we worked with transparency. Our vision statement was a true reflection of all that makes up our positive school C.U.L.T.U.R.E.

Although Tony's story about revamping the vision statement is specific to Cantiague, it speaks to the idea that any leader who wants to nurture and spread a positive school culture must build relationships that are rooted in trust and respect. These relationships are the impetus for effective communication, which is critical to school culture. We must be consistent and clear in communicating our sense of the culture to all members of the school. Creating a constant flow of information operates as a kind of formative assessment that will allow us to self-correct missteps and reinforce the best aspects of the school, leading to a durable and positive culture. School leaders who are transparent develop relational trust because communities respond to strong, consistent messages that are visible to everyone. Kids, families, and teachers will trust a school leader who helps them understand what he or she is doing and why, and who demonstrates actions that clearly serve the best interest of kids.

These relationships, high levels of trust, and cultural norms should then be communicated throughout the school and beyond it to ensure that the entire community shares a common vision. Be sure to clearly articulate the culture you want to create by rewriting and redefining the school vision statement. One of the first tasks given to those of us in a leadership position is to consider the vision statement for our school. You know what we are talking about: that bulleted list of generic phrases and words schools use to try and capture what the schooling experience will be like for its children. Here is an example, in case it's been a while since you looked at your own vision statement:

> *Our vision is that children leave school with:*
> *A set of values—being honest, being determined, and being considerate of others.*
> *A set of basic skills—literate, mathematical, scientific, artistic, and social.*
> *Strong self-esteem and developed self-confidence. Tolerance and respect for others.*
> *We value the partnership which exists between school, families, and our community in realizing this vision.*

Those sound like some pretty wonderful, important aspects of a child's development. But what is the point of this vision statement? What does it really mean for a school community? As you consider your school's C.U.L.T.U.R.E. make sure that it is undergirded by the school's vision statement, which should be personalized to your community and reflect common hopes, goals, and dreams for your students.

The school leader embodies a school's culture. Its leader's words and actions represent a school's priorities and concerns. We get a sense of culture when we witness a school leader:

- get down on the floor and smile while interacting with a group of first-graders,

- help a teacher navigate a difficult situation without passing judgment or controlling every aspect of the situation,

- patiently listen to and support an upset family member without reacting or getting defensive,

- take stakeholders' opinions into account when implementing policies.

We see a source of culture in the profound influence a school leader has on the community.

You just read
Hack 2: Create C.U.L.T.U.R.E.
from

Read more at Amazon.com

HACKING ASSESSMENT

TEACH STUDENTS TO SELF-GRADE

Put the power of grading into students' hands

Life will never be close enough to perfect, and listening
to that voice means stepping outside of yourself and
considering your own wrongdoings and flaws.
— ASHLY LORENZANA, AUTHOR

THE PROBLEM: GRADES ARE SUBJECTIVE

WHEN A GRADE is calculated by averaging tests, projects, homework, and class participation, the teacher often has only a cursory understanding of a student's actual learning. Even if the teacher has observed the student at work, what he or she sees is only part of the picture. Many times teachers think they know what students know and can do, but misjudge the reality. If we don't include students in the evaluation process, we are missing a vital piece of the puzzle.

Too often a teacher's bias plays a role in how students are graded. This prejudice is human, but unjust. For example, how many times has a student's reputation distorted your impression, even before you met him or her? Does a student's behavior change the way you read his or her work? Aren't there some kids you just like more than others, even though you'd never admit it?

- What teachers see is not always the full picture.

- Grades can be affected by prejudice.

- Leaving students out of the grading process denies students the right to show what they truly know and can do.

THE HACK: TEACH STUDENTS TO SELF-GRADE

Since traditional grades misrepresent learning, it is essential to teach students how to self-evaluate based on a set of standards or class expectations. We must give them the ability to look objectively at their bodies of work and determine their own levels of mastery by using evidence from their learning.

WHAT YOU CAN DO TOMORROW

Teaching students to self-evaluate will take time but that doesn't mean you can't get things started now. Here are some things you can do right away:

Stop grading student work without student input. What you see on the page and what is in a student's head may be different, so there is a better way. I understand that logistically it may be easier to grade alone at times, but we must bear in mind what is most beneficial for students. Grading fatigue can happen, too, when grading alone. The more time we spend looking at the same assignment, the less consistent our opinions become. The students at the top of the stack usually get the best of us, while those at the bottom could potentially get a cursory read.

Introduce the difference between reflection and self-evaluation to the students. As with the no-grades mindset, this will take a little convincing, but starting with a conversation about why students will be evaluating themselves helps to grease the wheel. Students also need to understand that while reflection is about the process of learning, the hows, whats and whys, the self-evaluation is the end result of that. Understanding the level of mastery achieved is the end result of the process demonstrated throughout the learning. Now the child must decide if he or she has met his or her goal.

Help students develop their own self-assessment tools. The key here is to do it with the kids and not alone. Single point rubrics work well. You can create one by making three columns on a piece of paper. Place the skills or content in the center and leave the columns on either side blank so students can fill them in to indicate their level of proficiency. On the right they will note areas of concern and on the left they will show areas that exceed standards. Students fill in evidence on either or both sides, based on the standard or skill. Or let kids group up to develop a rubric based on the standards the assignment asks them to address. Have them indicate proficiency by referring to specifics in the work they did.

A BLUEPRINT FOR FULL IMPLEMENTATION

Step 1: Discuss the new role students will play in the assessing process.

Students will need to have some kind of understanding of mastery learning when they have to grade themselves. Because you are no longer working with a point or letter scale, which is all they have known, you will need to provide them with something else to measure themselves by. You will need to help kids grasp mastery learning the same way you taught them about the no-grades mindset. Their understanding is key to their ability to assist in collaboration for their end "report card" if the school requires one. Essentially, they will be determining the grade with the teacher's support rather than the other way around.

Step 2: Provide a checklist to help scaffold the self-assessment process.

Students will need some guidance, especially at first, so either provide them with a basic checklist or generate one with their help to keep them focused while they assess. The checklist will need to include clear criteria that they are assessing themselves against. If they know what mastery looks like and in which areas they need to show it, that will streamline the process.

Step 3: Allow students to self-grade using evidence.

When students assess how they are doing, it's not good enough for them to say, "I deserve to be considered proficient because I know what I did." They need to be more specific, taking evidence from their work that supports their assessment. Often I tell students it's like writing an argument paper. You make an assertion about something and then you need to support the assertion with evidence from the text. In this analogy, the "text" is their assignment and this is where they draw their support from.

See below for an excerpt of exemplary student work. Anastasia Papatheodorou was a senior in my AP Literature and Composition class. She was one of my hardest sells about giving up grades and also one of my greatest success stories.

> For starters, I'll get straight to how I have done this term specifically. I most definitely had my lazy moments this term. Right when I was struck by the deadly senioritis, it came time for a fifteen-page research paper. That was definitely tough to get through, but I was pretty proud of myself after that. Although it still needed more work, I think that paper definitely showed an

improvement in development. As I mentioned in my last reflection, depth has been something I've struggled with all year, but I think this paper really showed how I started with an idea and I expanded on it. (Delineate and evaluate the argument and specific claims in a text, including the validity of the reasoning as well as the relevance and sufficiency of the evidence.)...

(specific evidence from her self-assessment was removed)

If I can take this class over I would want to continue to work on depth because I have improved, but just like with anything there is always room for improvement. I would want to focus on depth specifically because if there is any skill that will get you far in life it is being able to answer the question "Why?"

Well, it has come to that point that I dread so much talking about in conferences, which is why I chose to write about it instead. The grade I believe I deserve is an...wait for it...A. Not to say that I deserve an A just because, well who doesn't want an A, but I truly never worked so hard toward a class before to actually improve. I show clear growth in not just organization and cohesion but, thanks to you Ms. Sackstein, also public speaking, use of technology, researching, and most important, reflecting.

Step 4: Converse with students to determine a final grade if one is needed for the report card.

Once students have prepared to self-evaluate by going through their body of work, then it is time to discuss it with the teacher. The student should have gathered evidence and he or she should be certain of the evaluation. The teacher shouldn't drill the student, but rather listen attentively, asking clarifying questions to fill gaps. These conversations should take about five minutes. At the end, the student provides a grade that will go on the transcript or report card. Make sure to use the grade that is determined in the conversation; there should be no surprises.

If the teacher doesn't agree with the student, then a longer conversation needs to happen. It's important to talk it out. If in the end, the student really believes he or she deserves a particular grade, I'm inclined to say let him or her have it. After all, the grade itself doesn't mean very much. This happened a few times my first year, and it left me with an unpleasant feeling that I needed to address personally. Because of the traditional beliefs I held at that time, I felt uneasy allowing the student to have the grade. Despite this challenge, however, I did allow the student's grade to appear on the report card.

OVERCOMING PUSHBACK

People will say that teachers are the only ones qualified to assess or evaluate students, and therefore sharing this responsibility is lazy on behalf of teachers. I've already addressed how teachers are intimately involved with helping students to assess themselves, which sometimes is more work than simply giving a grade would be. It should be clear, too, how much students benefit from learning how to self-assess. This resistance seems to stem from another source of tension: How can we control the students if they have power over their own grades? Honestly, teachers and parents are the ones who need the grades. Grades are often used to motivate or punish, making them very powerful tools that both teachers and parents can use to get students to do things they may not want to do. This pushback isn't insurmountable.

All students would inflate or deflate their own grades. You'd think that, but most students are actually pretty honest, and those who aren't really just require a frank conversation. There is no shaming necessary—just ask a few questions and they will usually make the necessary adjustments. When students will not alter the grade (and they are very few), ask them to present their work and have them look at theirs next to an exemplar. Ask them to make comparisons. Ultimately the evaluation needs to come from them, so our job is to help them see what is in front of them objectively.

What about the student who does no work, but still thinks he or she should pass? Again, a frank conversation is in order here. Perhaps you talk to the student about what he or she knows. Believe it or not, just because work hasn't been completed, doesn't mean learning hasn't happened. We do need evidence of learning, but sometimes a conversation and alternative assignment can do the trick.

"But I don't want to give myself a grade." Some students may resist self-evaluation, and that is probably because they don't feel confident in what they see and feel about themselves. It is important to help students understand that they are the only ones who truly know what they know and understand. If they don't want to work alone to develop their evaluation, partner with them and help them build their confidence. You may hear things like, "I hate this part" or "I don't like grading myself." I usually answer with, "I don't like grading you either; that's why we're doing it like this. This grade isn't a measure of what you know and can do, it is just a formality."

How can I allow this student to get this grade? Okay, so here's a tricky one. You may find that you have some conflicting feelings about putting the control into the student's hands. I'd be lying if I said there weren't one or two conferences where I really didn't agree with what the students said, and despite my best effort to help them understand my view, they held their positions. I needed to take a breath and remember that the grade isn't important and if this was the level students really believed they had attained, I had to trust them as much as I trust the process. Be patient and try to move past the "justice" reflex. It's not about fairness; it's about mastery achievement.

> It's time to pass the baton to the students and watch in amazement as they skillfully share what they have learned.

THE HACK IN ACTION

Perhaps the greatest trepidation I had this year was placing the responsibility for final grading into my students' hands. Like most educators, I was used to handling the burden on my own (and I think I secretly liked to have the power), but grading had come to seem arbitrary and tiresome, and so when it came time to test the effectiveness of our changes in tracking achievement, it was only fitting that the students assumed control of their grades, just as they had managed other aspects of their assessments.

First, I sent out a survey to see how students would like to communicate their final grades. They could choose to share them in writing, on Voxer with an audio file, on video or screencast, or in a one-to-one conference. Once I got a preliminary idea of how many students were going to do what, it was time to provide some instruction about the expectations.

Preparing for final self-assessments - directions

It's the end of year and now it's time to really think about what you've learned. In preparation for your end of the year self-assessment, I'd like you to prepare a bunch of things...

Since there are several options for how you can present it (already signed up for) read the general information and then only the part that specifically refers to your delivery method.

General directions:
You will prepare your evidence of learning to show what you have mastered or at least become proficient in.

1. Review the standards specific for your class
2. Review your work completed this year and the reflections
3. Determine which work shows your mastery against the standards
4. You should be able to show your learning in each of the core groups of learning with specific reference to the assignments:

Reading	Speaking	Language
Writing	Listening	Technology

5. Make sure to indicate your areas of growth
6. Did you meet your goals for the year?
7. What do you feel you could have done better? Why? How would you change this?

If you are writing this out, make sure to comprehensively discuss the standards for each of the core areas and the assignments/projects that address each of the sections. Make sure to write it like a reflection with evidence from your work. Take screenshots to help show what you're talking about.

If you are using video, screencasting or speaking (Voxer or voice message), I recommend you plan what you're going to say first.

If you are having a conference with me, you must come prepared with above information and evidence. Think before you come.

The conference schedule will be given out over the next week for each class. Those of you doing an alternative form of reflection, your work is due on_____

Figure 9.1

The assignment sheet outlined specific deadlines so those students who were to meet with me face to face could prepare their evidence for the conference by the date we were scheduled to meet. My goal for having them prepare was to make sure students could show their mastery of the year-long standards by presenting evidence from their bodies of work. This avoids having any students arbitrarily inflate or deflate grades based on their feelings about learning in the class rather than their actual accomplishments. Whereas some students feel that they "deserve" a good grade regardless of their learning because they worked hard, some students believe that they "aren't good math students" or they are "humanities" people, and they downplay their achievements. Having them find specific evidence is a way of helping them be more objective and accurate.

As the written and video assignments began coming in, I realized quickly that I wasn't going to be disappointed with my choice to empower the students. Each display or written discussion of learning was cohesive, thoughtful, and evidence-based. Students had a candor in their writing and an honesty about growth and challenges that was most unexpected.

By the time I finished, I was completely impressed by how thorough students were. I had three students who believed they deserved to fail and gave me the reasons. Most students were spot on. Every child's assessment was what appeared on the report card. There were absolutely no surprises and no tears or angry emails on report card day.

Joy Kirr, a National Board Certified middle school English teacher, shared this example of how her seventh graders self-grade their reading.

> My students grade themselves on their independent reading. When the year begins, I ask each student to reflect on his or her reading habits each week. The first reflection sheet I give them asks them to evaluate six parts of their reading. Some students don't read an entire book, and most don't know how many pages they've read, but it gets the conversation going. The first few reflections do not go into the grade book, as we're practicing how to reflect (and I really don't care for grades).

How did you do this week on your reading? Circle any that are true.

1. I read for an average of 20 minutes (or more) at home each day.
2. I remembered to bring my book home each day and back to school in the morning.
3. I got right into the reading zone whenever I was given free reading time at school.
4. I was always reading a book I enjoyed.
5. I finished _____ book(s) this week.
6. I read _____ pages this week.

This is the grade I deserve for reading this week _____ **out of 5** because _____
_____
_____.

Figure 9.2

Still, some students are very hard on themselves. They'll give themselves a 9/10 because, "I finished it but not until the bus ride to school this morning" or "I really didn't try to understand parts that confused me." These make great discussion starters for one-on-one conferences. As the year moves forward, we continue with the reflection and new goal setting, whether it goes into the grade book or not. This reflection is the reason we are putting in all this time and effort; so students can see how they progress throughout the year.

It seems like no one enjoys grading, yet teachers are uncomfortable delegating the responsibility. We need to partner with our learners to create an environment where tracking progress and evaluating that process is transparent. It's time to pass the baton to the students and watch in amazement as they skillfully share what they have learned. Consider who does the grading now. How might you introduce self-evaluation into your practice? How might you model the activity for students? What impact would doing this kind of activity have on learning?

You just read
Hack 9: Teach Students to Self-Grade
from

HACKING
ASSESSMENT
10 Ways to Go Gradeless in a
Traditional Grades School

HACK
Learning
SERIES

Starr Sackstein

Read more at Amazon.com

PINEAPPLE CHARTS

Boost Teacher Collaboration with a Public Chart of "Open Door" Lessons

Alone we can do so little; together we can do so much.
— HELEN KELLER

THE PROBLEM: LITTLE TO NO PEER OBSERVATION

TEACHERS ARE CONSTANTLY searching for new ideas, solutions to problems with classroom management, organization, and instruction. "I need to figure out how to get my students to understand this concept," they say, or "I need to find someone who knows how to do ____." Time and money for professional development are both in short supply, but too often the most valuable resource—the teacher next door—is completely ignored.

The idea of observing other teachers is nothing new. It's the way we all first started learning how to teach, and you'd be hard-pressed to find a teacher who hadn't learned *something* from sitting in a colleague's classroom. Observing each other teach is one of the easiest and fastest ways to refresh our practice, learn new strategies, and build rapport with one another. And although many teachers say their door is always open, most of the time we never leave our own classrooms.

One reason for this is that everyone is busy—time is such a valuable commodity and no one has enough extra time to find out what another teacher is doing and plan a visit. The other reason is payoff: Even with the teacher whose door is always open, how do you know what she's doing on any given day? There's too much risk of showing up at the wrong time, interrupting something that really shouldn't be interrupted, or going all the way across the building, then settling in to observe a lesson that you quickly realize isn't all that relevant to you.

If only there were a way to see, at a glance, what other teachers are doing right now in your building. A way to know at a moment's notice whose door is open for observation and what's going on inside. A way to decide, if you have a few minutes to spare, where you might go to see some really interesting teaching.

THE HACK: POST A CALENDAR OF "OPEN HOUSE" LESSONS

The pineapple is a traditional symbol of welcome. When it's displayed on welcome mats and on door hangings, the intended message is "Come in! All are welcome here." A Pineapple Chart is a systematic way to put a "welcome mat" out for all classrooms, a central message board that lets other teachers know that you're doing something worth watching today, and if they'd like to come by, your door is open.

> What's even better is that this system is dynamic and customizable; it's the exact opposite of a one-size-fits all PD.

The chart would be something like a dry-erase board, sectioned off with tape or wet-erase marker into days of the week and class periods. The board would be kept near teacher mailboxes, the copier, or some other high-traffic area for staff. Every week, teachers would add their own classroom activities that others might like to see. These could be lessons in which the teacher is trying a new instructional strategy, when a new technology tool will be used, when students will be actively creating something, or even just when an interesting topic will be covered. This offers other teachers a menu of options for informal observations and allows them to visit places where they have a high interest.

🍍	Mon	Tue	Wed	Thu	Fri
1		Taylor: Reciprocal Learning			
2	Hughes: Socratic Circles			Silva: Video Editing in iMovie	Silva: Video Editing in iMovie
3		Vasquez: Ellis Island Simulation	Vasquez: Ellis Island Simulation		
4	Turner: Impressionism		Miller: Frog Dissection	Miller: Frog Dissection	
5				Wilson: Measuring heart rate	
6	Robertson: Poetry Slam	Patel: Kahoot quiz	Robertson: Discussion of Lord of the Flies		
7		Patel: Kahoot quiz			

Figure 2-1

When other teachers see something on the board, they know they have explicit permission to stop by that class during that period to informally observe. They can stay as long as they like—even just a few minutes—and when they're ready to go, they go. That's the end: No paperwork, no post-observation conference, just a visit to see what's going on in other classrooms.

This system offers endless possibilities for learning. Teachers might observe someone in their content area for specific strategies they can use themselves. They can also watch a class in a different subject or grade level to pick up ideas on classroom management, organization, or strategies that can be transferred across curricular lines. Some teachers might sit in on a class because the topic just interests them—how often have you heard people say they wish they could go back and take their high school history classes again? In some cases, a teacher who is trying something new or dealing with a difficult behavior issue might ask observers for feedback. And other times, observations might occur when a teacher just wants to see a friend teach—peer observation can be a true bonding experience.

What's even better is that this system is dynamic and customizable; it's the exact opposite of a one-size-fits all PD. Each week, teachers make their own decisions about what they need or are interested in. If they have a packed schedule for several weeks, they may not do any observing at all, but when time is available (or an especially interesting lesson motivates them to *make* time), they can take advantage of something that meets their own specific needs.

There's one more benefit to Pineapple Charts and peer observation: Having teachers join each other in the classroom sets a wonderful example of collaboration and lifelong learning for our students. When another teacher visits and students ask why, explaining the rationale sends the message that teachers are always looking for ways to learn and improve, and they're doing it together, just as they hope students will.

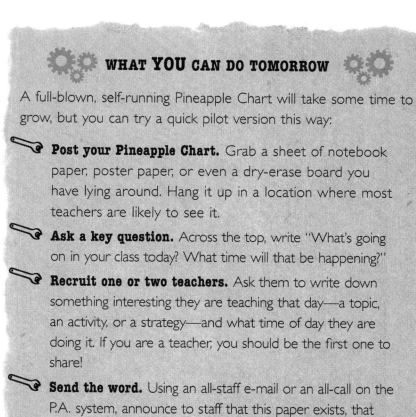

⚙️ WHAT **YOU** CAN DO TOMORROW ⚙️

A full-blown, self-running Pineapple Chart will take some time to grow, but you can try a quick pilot version this way:

Post your Pineapple Chart. Grab a sheet of notebook paper, poster paper, or even a dry-erase board you have lying around. Hang it up in a location where most teachers are likely to see it.

Ask a key question. Across the top, write "What's going on in your class today? What time will that be happening?"

Recruit one or two teachers. Ask them to write down something interesting they are teaching that day—a topic, an activity, or a strategy—and what time of day they are doing it. If you are a teacher, you should be the first one to share!

Send the word. Using an all-staff e-mail or an all-call on the P.A. system, announce to staff that this paper exists, that Ms. _____ is doing _____ in her room today and welcomes visitors, and encourage other staff members to add their activities to your makeshift Pineapple Chart.

A BLUEPRINT FOR FULL IMPLEMENTATION

Step 1: Set the stage.

Explain the overall process of the chart to the staff. This can be initiated by an administrator or a single teacher (with admin permission). Be clear that this is nothing like formal observations, where there can be job-related consequences. The point of the Pineapple Chart is to encourage everyone to share their ideas and practices with others.

Step 2: Create the chart.

Ideally, this would be a large whiteboard hung in a prominent location, with dry-erase markers readily available. (Think about those big surgery schedules you see on TV hospital shows.) Along the left-hand column, divide the chart by class periods or time-frames, however your school sets up its day. Across the top, divide the chart by the days of the week.

Step 3: Recruit early adopters.

For this to work, your school needs a team of enthusiastic participants to get things going. Privately recruit two groups: teachers who are not shy about having visitors in their classroom and are willing to add their names and activities to the chart when it's still a big blank space, and another group who will commit to making visits and talking them up with colleagues throughout the building. Have these teachers get the chart going, but be sure everyone understands that the chart is open to anyone.

Step 4: Encourage others to participate.

After the first wave has passed, it may be necessary to gently push others to join in. Although participation should be strictly optional, if you hear about a teacher who is trying something new in her classroom, suggest that she add the lesson to the chart. And if you know of a few teachers who never make observation visits, find one you believe would be a good fit for them and ask if they'd like to go with you.

Step 5: Make room for reviews.

Create time and space for teachers to share positive reviews of their visits. This can take many forms, like setting aside five minutes at the start of every faculty meeting to let people describe something great they saw that week, or adding a second board beside the Pineapple Chart where people can write or pin comments and reflections about specific visits.

Reflections might look something like this: "Go see the Cubist paintings in Heldic's room—amazing!" or, "Really enjoyed watching students play with Kahoot in Mr. Bowen's class today." Tech enthusiasts might reflect in a cloud-based location, like a shared Google Doc where people continually add their own comments about things they learned, or a "Database of Expertise," a spreadsheet where specific skills are listed (like flipping the classroom or cooperative learning) along with recommendations of people who are especially good at them.

Step 6: Incentivize it.

Over the long term, teachers could be given incentives for participation (as observers or hosts) in the form of professional development credit, being relieved of supervision duties ("10 visits = one day off bus duty!"), or other surprises, like the administrator brings you breakfast or a grab-bag of coupons from local businesses. These are marvelous ways to make professional development fun, and what teacher doesn't love fun PD?

OVERCOMING PUSHBACK

Making Pineapple Charts work well requires staff participation, and for some teachers, that means getting past these hurdles:

I'm too self-conscious to have people watch me teach. That's fine. Seriously. If some people never want to write their names on the board, don't pressure them. If this becomes something mandatory, people will resist. Those who are more shy about having visitors will still get a lot from going to watch other people teach. And if you emphasize and model positive feedback, and incentivize the program, eventually people will start to realize that only good things can come from the classroom visits.

I don't do anything interesting enough. Some people may get the impression that only the most innovative lessons are worth putting up on the board, and that they have nothing to offer. This is where your early adopters come in: Make sure that the first few people who put their lessons up include some things that might be considered ordinary. You never know what might attract someone. A basic lecture on Roman architecture might entice an art teacher who has a special interest in that topic. And your reputation for a beautifully organized classroom or creative discipline strategies might be the reason someone comes to your room—the topic might just give them an excuse to show up.

This is one more thing we have to do. No, it isn't. Remember, participating in Pineapple Chart visits is never mandatory. It's fun, simple, and optional. The draw to visit should come from the learning activities themselves, not pressure from administrators.

What if I visit someone's room and end up not liking it after a few minutes? Make it understood ahead of time that visits can be as short as five minutes or as long as a full class period. Be sure everyone is clear ahead of time that someone leaving after a short time doesn't mean your lesson isn't good; they might only have a few minutes, or they might not find it relevant.

Education unconferences like Edcamps have an understood "rule of two feet," where people are encouraged to get up and leave sessions whenever they decide the information is not relevant to them, and session leaders are strongly encouraged to leave their egos at the door and not take it personally! If your early adopters model a relaxed, truly open-door attitude, it will quickly become contagious.

I can't give up my planning time to observe another teacher. Indeed, everyone is short on time. That's just one more reason *not* to force teachers to visit. Since this is not a formal observation and you're not obligated to complete paperwork, it's perfectly fine to sit in the back of another teacher's room and grade papers or catch up on email; you can absorb a lot just by being in the room. Because this is not a formal observation, no one needs to give 100 percent attention to what's going on—you're there to pick up a few new ideas, get a feel for how someone else does things, see your students in a new light, and show an interest in what your peers are doing. If multitasking is the only way to make that happen, then multitask you must.

THE HACK IN ACTION

At Woburn Memorial High School in Woburn, Massachusetts, teachers began using the Pineapple Chart in the spring of 2015. "There was a ton of enthusiasm as soon as we shared the idea with the staff," says Abby Morton, the earth science teacher who introduced the chart. And not long after the chart was posted, teachers started visiting each other's classrooms.

Just as in the example above, Morton had to recruit a few of her fellow teachers to take the lead in signing their names to the chart, but soon other names appeared as well, and the visits began. "People always talked about wanting to see each other's lessons, but it's like so many other things in teaching—if you don't plan it, it doesn't happen."

Woburn's early experiences demonstrate the versatility and cross-curricular potential of the Pineapple Chart. One of the first visits was when an ESL teacher came to visit Morton's classroom to observe a science lesson. "I was struck by her open, comfortable teaching style, and in the way she encourages all to take part in the discussion," the visiting teacher reported. Despite the fact that the two work in different content areas, the visiting ESL teacher picked up some ideas that go beyond the curriculum.

Peer observation is one of the most powerful, affordable forms of professional development. By offering teachers an easy way to find the exact learning activities that interest them at a time that fits their schedule, Pineapple Charts make peer observation available to everyone, all the time.

You just read
Hack 2: Pineapple Charts
from

Read more at Amazon.com

TEACH THEM TO TINKER
Play Through the Process

It is a happy talent, to know how to play.
—Ralph Waldo Emerson, Poet/Lecturer

THE PROBLEM: WRITERS STRUGGLE TO
GENERATE AND DEVELOP CREATIVE IDEAS

A s a young teacher, I was perpetually hunting for perfect writing prompts, strategies, and tools, certain that if I asked the ideal question, provided the right graphic organizer, orchestrated the best set of strategies, I'd help my students generate and execute enticing ideas.

These efforts brought me some small measure of success. I could often get my kids writing, and when they followed my lead what emerged was often accurate, if uninspired. Getting them to persevere through the process was far more challenging than I ever imagined, though.

Eager to unlock the secret to sustaining their momentum, I began studying the writers who not only invested themselves from the start, but who maintained their stamina throughout the process. I noticed that these writers invested significantly more time in idea generation, and they often employed strategies that were different from those I taught them. It was clear that those who planned their writing struggled less; however, these same writers told me that the graphic organizers I required were confining.

My most invested writers were quietly but fiercely independent. They generated their own processes for accomplishing things, and they often kept this hidden from me. They were eager to please, but self-aware enough to know that pleasing me had little to do with their growth.

These writers often augmented the strategies that I provided or avoided using them altogether unless they were required to do so. They also made creative use of the resources at their disposal and sought out others on their own.

THE HACK: TEACH THEM TO TINKER

When we make writing, we tear things down, break them apart, build, test, and reconstruct as we go. Like makers, writers work with many moving, interdependent parts, and while our spaces are filled with containers that hold supplies, the containers we depend on most are those that house our ideas. These are the same containers that make our thinking and our knowledge visible. Tangible. Mobile.

More than any prompt, organizer, or strategy that I assign, the spaces, supplies, and tools I provide serve as catalysts for new ideas and remedies for the dilemmas that writers face. When I was a new teacher, my lessons helped students write efficiently and proficiently. My goals are very different now. Experience has taught me that talented writers are far more than efficient or proficient. They're adept.

CHARACTERIZING THE ADEPT WRITER

While many writers begin the process by sketching outlines and filling out graphic organizers, adept writers often begin by tearing other texts apart. They break down the work that inspires them, studying how it works so they can mimic an expert's approach. While these initial efforts might feel unsatisfyingly derivative, modifying existing frameworks typically inspires the development of texts that are legitimately original.

Writers who become adept are distinct in another way: Rather than approaching the process as a routine or a set of defined steps, they move through it in a recursive fashion. Most notably, they *tinker* during each phase of the writing. When writers tinker, they often make their writing moveable, crafting it on index cards or sticky notes, slicing their drafts into pieces, and isolating portions of their work from the whole in order to study and play with them.

Approaching writing as a continuous process forwarded by efficient movement from one step to the next often fails to help writers discover anything new about themselves or their work. If they are to remain invested, novice writers need to reap far greater rewards. Deep processing satiates, and tinkering is what enables it.

Adept writers are not satisfied by plans that result in the tidy production of drafts. They strive to surface the unexpected, and they generate multiple ideas and options before selecting the best path. They aim for complexity, playing with the possibilities that emerge from the process, often shaping and reshaping their vision as they draft deeper into their work. These writers go well beyond merely getting the job done.

This is how magic happens, and magic is what writers are after. They get it. Writing isn't merely a means to an end such as publication. Writing is a richly rewarding end in itself. Tinkering empowers writers to elevate the quality of their writing as they go. This is how they become expert craftsmen.

Revisiting the Writing Process

A writer's recognition of alternative approaches and eagerness to test and learn from them may account for some distinction between adept and less dexterous writers. To foster this understanding, we can begin simply by questioning the most popular models of the writing process and casting a critical eye over what these models make visible versus what remains concealed.

In its traditional form, the writing process appears to be linear: prewriting, drafting, revising, editing, and publishing. While such a model conceptualizes writing simply and clearly, it is decidedly misleading and has provoked serious misinterpretation. The process is not sequential, nor is it tidy, and when writers are initiated into their work in this way, the expertise they gain is likely superficial at best.

Other renditions of the process liken it to a synergistic web rather than a series of steps. While these models promote a more accurate representation of the process, they fall short in another significant way: They only lay the surface of it bare. The magic of the process remains concealed.

Familiarity with writers and writing has taught me that there is no one way to experience the writing process. It is a multifarious and ever-shifting enterprise. While models can help us develop a sense of what happens for most writers, they cannot represent the various ways individual writers move into and out of phases, nor do they establish set patterns for the actions and types of thinking writers do during the process.

I've learned that much can be gained from asking writers to define and sketch their own models rather than imposing one on them. Consider your own process: What does it typically look like? Do you always begin by brainstorming ideas, or do you prefer to leap right into drafting? Are you a planner, or do you prefer to let your stories surprise you? I share my own process before I ask such questions, in order to distinguish doodling and sketching from pursuing high art. Since my intention is to support rather than direct writers, asking them to make their processes transparent is a powerful entry point into that work.

This approach helped me discover something important: It's interesting to compare how writers move from one state in their processes to the next, but what happens at the intersection of states is incredibly compelling, and so is the transformation in thinking that I witness when writers strive to make what happens there apparent.

Writing can sometimes seem like an ethereal endeavor, but self-awareness makes us masters of our own experiences. The most masterful and satisfied writers I know share one commonality: Regardless of how they approach the process, when they speak about what happens in the intersection of states, their descriptions are reminiscent of tinkering.

What's tinkering?

Tinkering with writing involves messing around with one small excerpt or one experience in the process, testing various strategies or approaches before committing to any one of them, and often experiencing happy surprises along the way.

When we tinker, we approach writing as an act of discovery. Our intent isn't to merely master craft, but to illuminate the process, to uncover our relationship with it, and notice how our productivity, our artistry, and even our abilities to persevere are affected.

New writers are often taught that revision takes place after drafting. Some distinguish it from editing, but many do not, and the resulting thinking and work are often less than gratifying. Approaching writing as a continuous process forwarded by efficient movement from one step to the next often fails to help writers discover anything new about themselves or their work. If they are to remain invested, novice writers need to reap far greater rewards. Deep processing satiates, and tinkering is what enables it.

Tinkering happens in each state of the writing process, regardless of how we move through it. The process can be recursive or even repetitive, depending on the level of satisfaction writers gain as they work it. Sometimes we need to revisit certain parts and work them differently to achieve the result we're hoping for. At other times, we need to cycle through most states multiple times. This requires patience on the part of the writer and restraint on the part of the teacher.

I've found it necessary to adjust my expectations, particularly concerning the production of original work, which requires scaffolding. In other words, the first time through a process, writers might rely heavily on the ideas and inspiration they gained from reading another writer's works. They practice creative theft, stealing with integrity, and modifying existing texts and frameworks to create their own. As writers gain experience and have the opportunity to tinker and test varied approaches, their ideas and the resulting text transform into authentic expertise.

A variety of tools enable this evolution, including index cards, sticky notes, notebooks, interactive charts, paper scrolls, foam boards, and grids. The purpose is to isolate ideas so we can move them around and situate them beside one another, creating new contexts and possibilities.

Notebooks, binders, and mind maps are important containers for independent writing efforts. Meaningful spaces, interactive displays, and anchor charts enable collaborative learning and play. Writers consistently participate in both kinds of experiences. Sticky notes and index cards enable transport, too: When writers record the thoughts, ideas, and bits of knowledge generated in one experience onto sticky notes, they are able to lift and drop them into another, making unexpected connections and realizing new potential.

A variety of digital tools contain and enrich our efforts to make writing as well. For instance, many writers and makers maintain blogs where they share snippets of their thinking and their work with others. They connect digitally with writers beyond our community to receive feedback and expand their learning networks.

Some students curate resources online, relying on social book-marking tools like Diigo to organize, archive, and share links to the digital texts that inform their work. They create Livebinders for similar purposes. Pinterest and FlickR allow users to communicate visually, and we've been using them in increasingly inventive ways. Online tools also inspire all kinds of making. As dynamic and empowering as these tools are, we find that they tend to supplement rather than supplant the containers we build out of composition books, sticky notes, file folders, and paper.

WHAT **YOU** CAN DO TOMORROW

- **Show writers how to tinker.** Begin by helping them select just one lens through which they will examine their own writing. Perhaps they'll study idea development, organization, voice, sentence fluency, word choice, character development, or using conventions for effect. Invite writers to dip into their drafts and lift out examples of the identified element. These small bits of text can be added to a writer's notebook, a new document on their laptops, or sticky notes. Once these bits are isolated, writers strive to revise them in a variety of ways. Inspiration can be gained from the work of authors who have demonstrated real craftsmanship. It's empowering to write like those we admire. Once writers have tinkered around with their writing in this way, they can invite others to review their adaptations and provide feedback. This input will help them choose the versions they will keep.

- **Introduce writers to tinkering routines.** Routines keep messy learning productive. They also help us make our thinking, learning, and processes increasingly visible. This is how communities of writers learn from one another.

The tinkering routines below are our favorites at the WNY Young Writer's Studio. They were inspired by Dave Gray, Sunni Brown, and James Macanufo, who wrote the book, *Gamestorming*. Some writers work with them independently, while others use them to engage in collaborative thinking.

Routine 1: Tinkering with Ideas

This routine prompts writers to consider how they might produce timely pieces that serve a wider audience well.

Timing: Writers benefit from this routine as they begin conceptualizing new projects. It's at this moment, long before drafting begins, that they determine what they want to say, who they want to say it to, and what forms their writing could take.

Goal: This routine helps writers choose meaningful purposes and audiences and appropriate genres. As they consider the turning points they've experienced in their own lives and the important lessons they learned as a result, potential topics begin to emerge. After they've refined their purpose and topic, they will enter into a second round of thinking to identify an audience. The third and final round helps them determine the most appropriate genre.

Group size: 1-3 writers

Duration: Approximately 40 minutes

Materials Needed: Board or chart, sticky notes, pens, optional prompts

Routine:

1. Each writer begins by drawing a timeline and a 3x2 matrix on a board or chart. Each axis should be labeled as follows (see image 3.1):
    Left Column: Self
    Center Column: Other
    Right Column: Self and Others
    Top Row: Relevant
    Bottom Row: Irrelevant

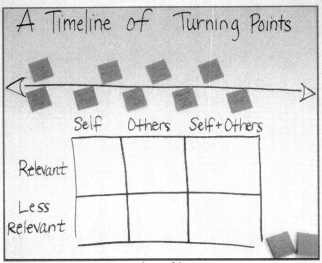

image 3.1

2. In round one, each writer uses sticky notes and pens to brainstorm turning points in his or her own life. Place one turning point on each sticky note, leaving space for additional note taking. Writers may brainstorm in response to prompts, if needed. They are provided in the variations section below.

3. Once writers have generated a set of turning points, they will reflect on the lessons that they learned from each experience and record them on the sticky notes below the defined turning points.

4. Next, writers will place their sticky notes on their matrixes by considering whether the

lessons remain relevant to them alone, to others alone, or to them and others now.

5. Once writers have completed their matrixes, the second round begins. Acting as reviewers, players will move in carousel fashion and explore the ideas generated by their peers.

6. Reviewers will indicate which ideas possess personal relevance by placing stars on the appropriate sticky notes. Then they will consider other audiences who might find the lessons relevant and list them by name on the appropriate sticky notes.

7. When writers return to their own matrixes, they will use the findings shared by their peers to refine their purposes and determine their audiences, keeping in mind that an ideal purpose is one that is both satisfying to the writer and relevant to others.

8. During the third round, writers will articulate their purpose and audience at the top of a new chart. Alternatively, place a sticky note in an empty space that allows for further idea generation, and write the purpose and audience on it.

9. Acting as reviewers, writers will move in carousel fashion from one chart to the next, considering each player's purpose and audience and then brainstorming potential genres, which they will record on sticky notes and place below the stated purpose and audience.

Variations:

A. If writers struggle to define turning points, they may reflect on the following prompts orally or through free writing:

Describe a time when your life changed because you:

- Said yes or no
- Listened to your heart or your head
- Stayed or left
- Spoke up or remained silent
- Played big or small
- Risked something or played it safe
- Agreed or disagreed
- Loved someone or remained distant
- Kept something or gave it away
- Won or lost

B. Rather than inviting reviewers to list all potential audiences at once in step 6, players could mention one idea at a time in rounds. This would prevent any one player from dominating idea generation and creating a list so lengthy that others struggle to contribute.

C. Writers could share their matrixes in other settings and invite people other than the initial players to contribute ideas.

D. Once writers determine their purposes, audiences, and genres, they could archive remaining ideas in their writer's notebooks for potential use in the future.

E. As writers complete step 9, some may produce ideas that are far more thoughtful than others. To encourage quality idea generation, invite writers to move beyond merely naming a genre. Challenge them to share specific ideas about the form that each piece could take.

F. Writers may choose to share their matrixes online via their blogs, Google Docs, or social networks. This will allow them to tap the perspectives of a far wider audience.

Norms:

1. The routine unfolds in silence, and writers may not qualify or defend their choices.

2. The teacher should let it be known that the intention of this routine is to generate as many ideas as possible, and since writers are not required to act on the ideas shared with them, they should move through the game quickly, wasting no time debating with others or defending their ideas.

3. Writers must wait until others have finished recording their ideas at a station before they begin adding their own.

Routine 2: Tinkering with Organization

"I know what I want to say, but I don't know how to say it."

If you're a writing teacher, I'm sure that you're no stranger to this frustration. It's one that I've always found particularly difficult to bear witness to, largely because I don't know what they want to say, and I can't help them begin to say it until these ideas are made clear. I find that when the writing process includes opportunities for writers to capture and then display the fragmented ideas that are swirling around inside of their minds prior to evaluating or attempting to organize them, determining how to say what they want to say becomes far easier.

Timing: This routine helps writers release and then organize abundant and even conflicting ideas. Left unchecked, these seeds of inspiration begin to grow and bounce around inside their minds, creating noise, soaking up their cognitive reserves, and depleting their creative energies. In short, they get stressed out. Routines like this help writers harness the chaos and use it in service of greater purposes.

Goal: This routine challenges writers to dump all of their ideas on the table, regardless of form or state of completion. Every bit counts. Once ideas are visible, writers begin clustering and categorizing them, noticing connections, trends, and often the unexpected. As the routine draws to a close, writers use their established categories and the ideas assembled in them to experiment with potential organizational structures.

Group Size: 1-3 writers

Duration: 40 minutes

Materials Needed: Board or chart, sticky notes, pens

Routine:

1. Writers begin the first round by recording all of their potential writing ideas on sticky notes (one idea per note). Display completed notes in random fashion on a board or a chart or in an open space.

image 3.2

2. Next, writers review their sticky notes, looking for potential connections between ideas. They cluster their ideas based on these discoveries.

3. During the second round, writers grab a stack of blank sticky notes and generate labels for each cluster. Record these category labels on

single sticky notes and place them above the cluster they refer to.

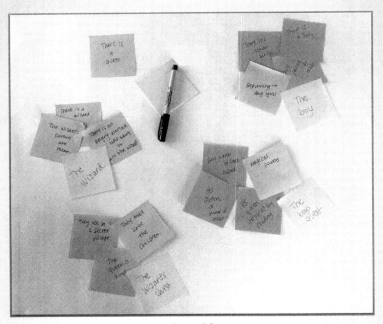

image 3.3

4. Next, writers review the ideas in each category, remove those that they are certain they will not use (these ideas could be archived for future use), and add new ideas as they emerge.

5. The last round of play challenges writers to organize their categories. Which category will they attend to first in their drafts? Why? How will it connect to those that follow?

Writers will order, reorder, and imagine varied structures for their pieces as they tap into the potential gained by making their ideas not only visible, but moveable.

Variations:

A. Writers may choose to engage others in this routine by inviting them to cluster and categorize ideas. Considering varied points of view often gives rise to new connections, ideas, and possibilities.

B. Work can continue long after time is called, especially if writers are able to store their sticky notes on a transportable board, in notebooks, or in file folders.

A BLUEPRINT FOR FULL IMPLEMENTATION

Step 1: Expect writers to explore multiple models and mentor texts. Writing teachers have a long history of relying on mentor texts to demonstrate different elements of a writer's craft. It's important to explore multiple models with writers if we hope to coach creative thinking. When I use a single mentor text, writers tend to emulate it almost exactly. When I vary my models, their writing becomes far more eclectic.

Step 2: Teach writers how to commit creative theft. Begin by inviting writers to find a few writers whose works are worth emulating. Ask students to study these pieces using a specific lens. Rather than merely annotating parts of the text, I recommend that writers cut them right out of their pages. Once they've gathered a small pile of inspirational excerpts, they should tinker around with what they see and add their own ideas. Students thus create something entirely new that is influenced by someone else's impressive writing. We all stand on the shoulders of giants: Teach writers to elevate rather than replicate. The anchor chart in image 3.4 illustrates this process.

image 3.4

Step 3: Teach them to tinker through the entire process. Great writers revise throughout the entire writing process. They tinker through it as well. Rather than presenting revision as a single step in a linear procedure, help writers embrace it for what it is: a constant part of a writer's thought process. Tinkering allows writers to break the text they are revising into small bits. This makes revision less daunting. It also makes our text mixable. This is how writers gain new insights.

Step 4: Tinker through your mini-lessons. As you plan your next mini-lesson, ask yourself where you might model a bit of tinkering. Which small pieces of your own text can you isolate and revise a few different ways for effect? Model this for your students. It will encourage them to try it themselves.

Step 5: Design tinkering routines beside writers, and challenge them to create their own. Use the examples I've shared as models for your own routines. Design them in response to the needs and interests of your students. Help writers identify problems that need to be overcome, and work with them to craft routines that can help them resolve these issues.

Step 6: Improve the frequency and quality of the feedback writers receive. Don't wait for them to finish a draft before you provide feedback. Try to peek over their shoulders during every writing experience and offer a bit of criteria-specific insight that relates to the skills you modeled during that day's lesson. Show them how to revise bit by bit as they go in response to your input.

OVERCOMING PUSHBACK

Tinkering takes too much time. We can ask writers to produce things quickly, and give kids superficial practice with a wider variety of genres, or we can invite writers to study and produce fewer genres of superior quality. The first approach will leave you certain that you covered your curriculum and produced numerous grades for reporting time. The second approach will leave you feeling more confident about the growth your students have made as writers.

Writers don't know how to use multiple approaches. This lack of knowledge is typical of novice writers, and it's why using multiple models and mentor texts is so important. Study texts with the intent to uncover the approach that the writer may have taken. Read writing blogs and articles that focus specifically on craft, sharing them with the writers you support. Encourage writers to play. Remind them that perfection isn't the goal: It's the problem that typically prevents most writers from testing multiple approaches.

I need to teach writers formulas that will give them success on standardized tests. When kids aren't writing well on the test, it's typically because they aren't doing enough authentic writing and learning about writing all year long. They don't understand how writing works, who they are as writers, or how to approach specific forms. Writing for the test has less to do with mastering a formula than with knowing how to frame a coherent, evidence-based response to a specific question. Agile writers do this well, and they can also transfer what they've learned to other experiences. Formulas don't build agility; experience and experimentation do.

THE HACK IN ACTION

"I have too many ideas," she sighed, sitting back and sinking deep into her chair. "They're all little bits and pieces and fragments of thoughts, swirling around in my head. I don't even know where to begin."

Helping writers embrace this sort of discomfort is one of my greatest challenges. After all, it's far easier to provide assignments, graphic organizers, and directive feedback. Compliance inspires a dangerous sort of certainty, though, and it usually results in mediocre work. Those bits and pieces and fragments of thought are fabulous content just waiting to be molded into shape. The more writers simply do what teachers tell them to do, the less they are able to generate and execute their own ideas or solve their own problems. This is how I discovered the power of the sticky note.

Lake Shore teacher Kristina Lewis uses sticky notes to help her students conduct research and use evidence to write informational texts. They gather isolated bits of evidence on single sticky notes as they investigate varied texts. They add their own ideas to separate sticky notes as well. Writers fill their desks and table tops with their discoveries, and then they cluster and categorize them. Categories become topics, and the notes enable writers to easily determine effective sequences for their drafts. A quick glance at their clusters helps writers identify which topics need further investigation, and it is possible to remove topics from the running entirely without losing them altogether.

The high school students I coach use sticky notes to tinker with their drafts, placing small extracts of writing on single notes and then using others to revise the extracts in multiple ways. They tinker with these alternatives, placing them into their drafts temporarily and testing the effect they have on the whole. This helps them think critically about their writing to make purposeful choices.

I've learned that there is no single "right" way to tinker with a text. It involves experimenting, sharing our varied iterations, and gaining feedback and perspective from potential readers. Tinkering is one of the very best ways to make writing. When writers share how they tinker, our own approaches shift in response. This is what creative writing means to me now.

You just read
Hack 3: Teach Them To Tinker
from

Read more at Amazon.com

HACKING ENGAGEMENT

HASH OUT A HASHTAG

THE PROBLEM: STUDENTS RARELY THINK ABOUT YOUR CLASS OUTSIDE OF SCHOOL

PICTURE THIS, ONE of your students is at home watching TV. Like most multi-tasking teens, he is scrolling through his phone while watching. Because he follows you on Twitter, your recent post pops up on his feed.

 Sturtevantclass @sturtevantclass · Apr 15
#heywc1...How about a slice of Buddha Bread with vegan butter? Can't wait 2 c what u make this weekend!

Image 14.1

He reads your tweet and laughs to himself, *Mr. Sturtevant is always putting bizarre things on our class hashtag* (see an example in Image 14.1). He likes your post, retweets it, and then remembers, *Oh yeah, I'm supposed to create a conscious eating Buddhist meal for our next blog prompt.* After reading your lighthearted electronic reminder, he waltzes into the kitchen and starts bouncing menu ideas off his mom. Mom shoots him a puzzled look, then asks him why, all of a sudden, he's interested in food prep. Instead of answering, he hands her his phone, which is displaying your class hashtag feed. She smiles as she scrolls through the tweets. She pauses on a post and then clicks on the embedded link for the Buddhist meal assignment. She reads the prompt and says, "I can see why you enjoy this class." After mother and son agree to a meal plan, your student replies to your tweet. He includes the hashtag #heywh1, so his friends will see it on the hashtag feed.

An engaging presence on Twitter can inspire kids to think, plan, and wonder about your class during their daily twenty-three-hour hiatus. It can expose your amazing classroom to grateful parents. It's time to morph your classroom into an online presence.

THE HACK: CREATE A TWITTER HASHTAG FOR YOUR CLASS

Please, if you haven't already, create a Twitter account for your class. Make it simple, but recognizable, like mine: @sturtevantclass. Think

Image 14.2

of a hashtag as an attention-grabber. Post general classroom announcements on the account feed, but if students are to reply, vote, or participate in a poll, include an attention-grabbing hashtag.

My hashtag is #heywc1. The class is World Civilization 1 and I want their attention, so I included the word "hey." Search Twitter to make sure your tag is original. If it's not, start from scratch. Here were options I considered for World Civilization 1:

- #sturtwc1
- #Wuzupwc1
- #thesturtfeed
- #attentionwc1
- #Yowc1

I like #heywc1 best. I include it on any tweet that encourages a response.

In *Hacking Engagement* podcast Episode 11 (Image 14.2), I share a story remarkably similar to my creation in this hack, including an interview with a student and a parent about the engaging nature of the activity.

WHAT YOU CAN DO TOMORROW

- **Create a class Twitter account.** This will keep your professional life and private life separate, which is always smart.
- **Create a unique hashtag for your class.** Create a tag that's relatively short, but it must be unique.
- **Promote the hashtag to your students.** In the beginning you'll have to lead them. Display the hashtag on the Smart Board and encourage kids to respond. After some days of successful participation, you can foster curiosity with an offhanded comment, "Check for an interesting class hashtag prompt."

> - **Share the hashtag with parents and administrators.**
>   Most teachers have some sort of online classroom.
>   Broadcast the hashtag to parents. Encourage them
>   to follow you and tweet to your hashtag. Email your
>   principal and guilt her into responding to the hashtag
>   prompt.
>
> - **Invite class alumni to join your hashtag.** Sturtevant
>   veterans add to the virtual conversation immensely.

A hashtag is a fantastic way to engage kids when they're not sitting in your classroom. It also creates a unique channel that brings parents and other stakeholders inside your world.

You just read
Hack 14: Hash Out a Hashtag
from

Read more at Amazon.com

HACKING LITERACY

SPOTLIGHT READING IN YOUR SCHOOL

That first follower is what transforms a lone nut into a leader.
— DEREK SIVERS, ENTREPRENEUR

THE PROBLEM: READING CULTURES EXIST IN ISOLATION

THIS CHAPTER DETAILS an important last step that is not as easy as managing your own classroom, but holds equal importance to the goal of hacking literacy.

Transforming students from non-readers to book lovers requires persistence and dedication. Each year as I build momentum for the reading culture in my classroom, I see small victories when students finish their books at home, read more books than they ever have, or discuss their reading choices with classmates. This success motivates me to keep following the process: give book talks, conference with students, help the reluctant reader find the book she will love. While I have confidence that my students' reading skills and enjoyment increase significantly in my class, I worry that their success will get derailed after they leave me.

As the hacks in this book illustrate, the actions required to build a culture of reading are simple, yet they must become habitual if teachers are to create lifelong readers. Literacy instruction reaches its maximum effectiveness when students are part of a culture of readers year after year, and when the whole school participates in a culture of reading. This is the true goal of hacking literacy: making literacy integral to everyday school life so that reading forms an indelible component of students' identities.

One obstacle to initiating school-wide reading culture is that teachers can only control influences in their own classroom environments. Few teachers work in a dual supervisor/teacher role, and many do not have the opportunity to share ideas with their colleagues through professional learning communities or other collaborative work groups. While one teacher is creating a thriving reading culture, another might be teaching students in a reading desert. This difference could be attributed to honest ignorance on the part of the teacher. He may not recognize or be exposed to the practices that foster a culture of reading in the classroom. But this lack of consistency undermines the goal of getting students to make reading part of their school lives and part of their identities.

THE HACK: SPOTLIGHT READING IN YOUR SCHOOL

Promote reading in every way possible beyond the doors of your classroom. Encourage teachers and students to share their reading lives with the school community. Hold events that prompt students to talk with each other and staff about books that they love. Make reading social by sharing meals over book discussions. Organize fun events that offer books as a reward, not a means to some other reward. Celebrate reading publicly; heighten its status to amplify its social acceptability. Make reading a cool thing to do. Integrate positive attitudes to reading and habitual reading practices into your school so that students get immersed in reading culture.

WHAT YOU CAN DO TOMORROW

- **Discuss reading culture with your school librarian.**
  The school library and librarian provide essential support for a school-wide reading culture. Talk to your school librarian about the reading culture that you are building in your classroom and discuss your hope to take the reading culture school-wide. Ask what initiatives the librarian has planned to promote reading and offer to collaborate to make them successful. Perhaps the library has acquired new additions that you can highlight to students and staff. You might promote the library's upcoming events with your students. You may have ideas to make the library a more inviting space for students to come to read. If your librarian seems open to suggestions, share your ideas to make the library a hub of school-wide reading culture. As with any complex

endeavor, this work cannot all be done tomorrow, but initiating dialogue is a positive first step. You will almost certainly find an ally in your quest to strengthen school reading culture.

- **Display your class's reading life on your door.** Exploit kids' natural curiosity about what happens in other classes to spread buzz about books outside your classroom. Ask your students to think of the title of a book that they have recently finished. Show examples of effective blurbs from the back of fiction and nonfiction books so they see how a short statement can capture a reader's feelings about a book. Hand out paper and instruct them to write their names and their book's title and author on the top of the page. Underneath, they write a one-sentence comment that encapsulates their experience with the book. Tape these short book reviews on your classroom door. Now every student in the school can see that your class is full of readers. The reviews will initiate book discussions between students in your class and their peers, and your colleagues will notice the reading culture you are building in your classroom.

- **Share your students' reading success on social media.** If you have a class Twitter, Facebook, Goodreads or other social media account, celebrate your students' reading accomplishments publicly. I started this practice by sharing my students' blog post reviews on Twitter, mentioning the authors of the books my students had reviewed. Your post might include the words, "Maria finished five books this quarter!" with a picture of the books stacked together. These posts do not need to contain pictures of students or their last names (and probably should not). Share success via social media with other teachers, staff members, and parents to reinforce students' efforts and to provide evidence that reading culture is thriving under your leadership.

A BLUEPRINT FOR FULL IMPLEMENTATION

Step 1: Transfer your reading activities to common school spaces.

Colleagues will be more likely to support your efforts at creating a reading revolution in your school if they know exactly what it looks like. Model effective reading culture by moving book talks and book passes to visible spots in the school, like the school library or other common areas. Both staff and students will be intrigued by the activities, presenting opportunities for you to spread the word about reading and possibly opening discussions about effective reading instruction.

Step 2: Share students' reading lives publicly.

One way to spread a culture of reading throughout a school is to provide opportunities for students to share their favorite books with the school community. This establishes reading as a normal activity for students, and can get kids talking to each other about their favorite books. One way to accomplish this is to have students write short reviews of their favorite books, and then post those reviews next to the physical copy of the book in the library. Students see that their writing has an authentic audience, and the library benefits from student book recommendations.

Step 3: Make reading the reward.

Some school-wide reading programs suggest that rewards incentivize students into reading more. Students win a pizza party if they read a certain number of books in a month, or they receive gifts like stickers and pencils for meeting reading accomplishments. Students may read more in the short term in such cases, but once the prizes disappear, so do the books. Rather than implying that only a reward would prompt a kid to read, spark interest in reading for its own sake. Make reading the reward.

Plan a book giveaway activity, where students have fun and receive books as prizes. You might consider a school-wide holiday book exchange, where students bring in a favorite book from home, wrap it up like a gift, then exchange the books in the library or another common area. Giver and recipient then have time to meet and discuss the book. You may decide if the books are kept or returned to their original owners. Rather than handing out certificates for good deeds, academic excellence, or other school honors, present book awards. When adults demonstrate that they consider books valuable by sharing interesting books as rewards, students will be more likely to value books themselves.

Step 4: Hold a "Literature Lunch."

Ask teachers in your school to nominate students to take part in a book club discussion during lunchtime. Choose a high-interest book that all participating students and staff will read by a certain date. Hold the discussion during the school's typical lunch period in a common area like a classroom. If your school has a culinary arts class, you might solicit their help in preparing the lunch. The food need not be special, though; students can eat their own bag lunches or bring food from the school cafeteria. When they participate in a discussion about a book with both staff and students in attendance, student perspectives on reading shift to view reading as lifelong adult readers see it. Reading belongs in all stages of life as a way to expand one's mind and engage in discussions with others about interesting stories and ideas.

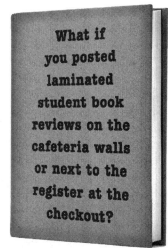

What if you posted laminated student book reviews on the cafeteria walls or next to the register at the checkout?

Step 5: Broadcast reading achievements on school television.

As students finish books, collect their names and the titles that they've read. For each, create an image on a PowerPoint or Google slide with the student's name, the title of the book, and a picture of the cover. Include a caption like, "Jane Doe just finished reading *The Hunger Games.*" Ask the audio/video department, or whomever is in charge of the school's closed circuit TV, to broadcast your slideshow whenever other announcements are not displayed.

Students will love seeing their reading accomplishments shared with the school community. Keep reading visible by celebrating student achievement to highlight its cool factor.

Step 6: Invite colleagues to participate in planning and organizing reading celebrations.

For a culture to sustain itself, its common knowledge has to be disseminated amongst all members of the culture. Although a leader can instigate change, others must participate to integrate these changes into the existing culture. Invite other teachers or administrators to hold their own reading celebrations in your school. Start small by asking one teacher to collaborate with you on an event, ask for input on a reading celebration, help someone else plan an activity. Encourage people to plan and implement future reading celebrations in the school. By involving others, you can ensure that the culture of reading in your school will live on into the future.

OVERCOMING PUSHBACK

Reading celebrations disrupt the atmosphere of the library. If noise is the issue, consider conducting a silent book pass in the library, or notify others by posting a sign on the library entrance or sending an email announcing that an activity will take place in the library that might be a little noisy. Be sure to include that all are welcome to participate. If using the library is the problem, invite teachers into your room to see how you do book passes and book talks, or perhaps conduct them in the hallway with students sitting on the floor.

The librarian is not interested in posting class projects. If the school librarian rejects your request to collaborate on a project like placing book reviews next to the books in the library, consider other alternatives. Brainstorm how you might display students' responses to their reading in other physical or digital spaces. What if each administrative office featured a hardcover copy of a book and a student's book review? What if you posted laminated student book reviews on the cafeteria walls or next to the register at the checkout? Could you create QR codes that link to student work and publish them in the school newspaper?

Others complain about too few or too many attendees. Sparse attendance often results from too little publicity. If, on the other hand, you're overwhelmed by attendees, you may suspect that many of them don't really want to participate in the activity, but have appeared as a way of escaping from class. Both of these issues could be solved through the same process: Ask teachers to nominate students to attend. The limited number of seats available makes the event special, and also gives the teachers the power to nominate students who will enjoy attending the event, approach it maturely, and benefit from it.

We don't have access to television in our school common area. Broadcast your celebrations on paper. Create a celebration wall using a large piece of poster paper or newsprint. Students use colorful markers to sign their names and write the titles of the books they have finished. You could also consider requesting the use of a trophy case or other display showcase to hang a sign displaying students' reading achievements.

THE HACK IN ACTION

This Hack in Action contains two stories, both from my home state of New Jersey. They show how a variety of the strategies shared in this chapter spotlight reading in a school.

Part 1: Amy Gazaleh

Amy Gazaleh, the librarian at Hightstown High School in New Jersey, has brought staff together to share their reading lives and has improved the physical space of the library to promote a culture of reading.

One change Amy made represents her stance toward student reading in a concrete way. She removed alarm sensors near the doors to create a more welcoming space. Previously, an alarm would sound if students left the library with a book that had not been checked out. The removal of the alarms was a philosophical decision about the importance of books in students' lives: "Entering the library by walking through security gates did not generate the message that this is a safe space in which everyone is welcome. I do not believe there is a problem with students stealing books—library books are free, after all—and those few that do steal them need them more than I do," Amy explains.

In addition to making the library a more welcoming space for students to come find books, Amy has promoted the culture of reading by inviting staff to share their reading lives with the school. At the beginning of the 2015-2016 school year, each teacher received a door sign for sharing their current reads. For example, mine says, "Mr. Dawson is reading…" with white space to fill in the title. Amy hopes the signs connect students with staff, and staff with each other: "The goal of the reading signs was to expand the reading conversation beyond the library and English classes. I want students to think about reading as a habit of mind, not an assignment, and to find common ground with someone in the building." Students often check out books from the library and explain to Amy that they discovered the titles from a teacher's door sign. The teachers' selections reveal interests that might not show in the classroom: science teachers read classics, history teachers read sci-fi, language teachers read historical fiction.

Amy has metaphorically blasted open the walls of the library to expand reading culture into the school. She visits classes to present book talks about thematically related texts that teachers have requested or new additions to the school library. For staff who want reading recommendations but struggle to find the time to search the library, Amy sends out a monthly "Book Blast" newsletter containing a list of thematically related books. In partnership with Mrs. Kudish, she has also created a staff book club, which had not previously existed. The idea behind this is simple, yet powerful: Every other month, teachers and administrators meet to discuss a shared book they have read. The books are either young adult fiction or nonfiction that might pique students' interests.

Part 2: Steve Ferguson and Christine Finn

Steve Ferguson is an English teacher at Cedar Creek High School in Egg Harbor City, New Jersey, and Christine Finn is the media specialist at Cedar Creek. Together, they've created a school-wide culture of reading through celebration and communication.

Steve and Christine created the hashtag #PiratesRead on Twitter as a way for students and staff to share conversations about books and communicate with authors. Steve explains that the hashtag was a simple way to build the culture of reading in their school: "The response from the students is positive, especially when they receive responses from the author or the author 'favorites' their tweet," Steve said.

Christine acknowledges the power that social media has for a school that wants to build public perception as a culture of readers. "We might not have the money for an author visit, but we can still give our students the opportunity to make a real world connection with writers. Tweets present doors to open conversations and to share interests which in turn builds rapport."

Steve and Christine have also started "Lit Lunch," a program where students eat lunch together and discuss a shared read. Culinary arts students prepare the lunch, the morning announcements TV show helps advertise the book selections, and teachers recommend the books. The collaboration between these groups helps emphasize the importance and celebration of reading in the school. The group meets for one and a half periods to talk about the book and eat together. Steve has observed diverse student perspectives being shared during Lit Lunches. "At times, it feels like *The Breakfast Club*. In fact, like *The Breakfast Club*, Lit Lunch allowed us to reach students who may not have otherwise found a group within the school community."

Steve and Christine show that giving students opportunities to discuss books, in person or online, extends the culture of reading in a school.

Make the reading in your classroom transparent to everyone else in the school, and then celebrate reading throughout the building. Involve as many of the other students, faculty, and staff as you can. Hold fun events that are centered around reading and talking about books to spread your culture of reading throughout the school.

You just read
Hack 5: Spotlight Reading In Your School
from

Read more at Amazon.com

HACKING HOMEWORK

AMPLIFY STUDENT VOICE

Incorporate choice in how kids learn at home

*"I never teach my pupils. I only attempt to provide
the conditions in which they can learn."*
—ALBERT EINSTEIN

THE PROBLEM: STUDENTS DON'T HAVE A
SAY IN WHAT AND HOW THEY LEARN

EDUCATION GENERALLY USES a top-down model, ignoring the most important voice—the student's. Administrators make choices about policy that don't embrace the teacher voice and then teachers make choices without hearing the student voice. We tend to rob students of decisions about their education and tell them what must be done, forcing them into compliance.

If education is truly about students, however, we must let students take ownership. The game of compliance doesn't inspire learning but quashes it, making critical thinking harder down the road. We want to make sure we take the opportunity to amplify student voice because:

- The less ownership we give students, the less they have the ability to think for themselves. They develop excessive concern for learning the "right" way, inferring that there is only one right way to learn. In reality, we have students with a variety of backgrounds and strengths, each one requiring something different. We can't lump them together and decide that one approach works for all.

- Learning should be a partnership, with the learner's needs central to decision-making. The expression of discontent in the form of non-compliance (not doing the work or copying someone else's) is an outcome of not involving students in the decision-making process.

- When we don't allow students to have a say, the purpose of the home learning is often unclear. It seems meaningless. Some students will follow teacher directions mindlessly but others won't. This dynamic jeopardizes the learning process.

THE HACK: AMPLIFY STUDENT VOICE; GIVE KIDS CHOICE

Once students understand what quality learning looks like both in and out of school, we can start involving them in decision-making, helping them make meaningful choices that deepen their learning. In this way, students are responsible for and invested in what they do. Since the work was their choice to begin with, the motivation to complete it is intrinsic.

Students must have some say about what they learn and how they learn it, especially when it happens at home. When given the opportunity to make choices about home learning, most students develop sound options; sometimes even better ones than teachers. If we want learning to extend beyond the day, we must offer students the chance to create learning on their own.

WHAT YOU CAN DO TOMORROW

- **Debate what quality looks like.** The more students are engaged in discussions about successful learning, the better you are able to understand their perceptions of learning and what they need to succeed. Listening to students' ideas about homework will help you give more effective assignments. Additionally, teachers can offer an exemplar and do a jigsaw in class, evaluating different assignments for home and then developing a checklist of the qualities that make it meaningful from the model they are examining. This way, the list comes directly from student thoughts and engagement.

- **Teach students to design their own learning opportunities.** Instead of only one assignment for home, offer a "choose your own adventure" option in which students decide how to demonstrate their knowledge but still fulfill learning objectives. It's good to have students get ideas approved at first, which also gives teachers the opportunity to provide immediate feedback on what students come up with. If the students do a great job (which they often do), then offer student ideas to the whole class as options for the future. Saying yes is much more gratifying than saying no.

- **Accept a variety of submissions.** Perhaps one of the simplest things we can do is offer students a choice as to how the work they do at home gets submitted. Instead of providing only a worksheet or asking for work to be written in a Google Doc, take student preference into account when deciding on the "how." If students feel more comfortable undertaking the work in a certain medium, it's very easy for you to let them do so. Too often we say no as a function of habit, because we want to control the way everything looks and make sure students comply. This attitude turns some students off and even constitutes a missed opportunity for learning. So try to stay open when a student makes a suggestion.

A BLUEPRINT FOR FULL IMPLEMENTATION

Step 1: Dissect the design process.

In order for this all to work, students must fully understand how to create a meaningful home learning experience. Spend time in class teaching the backward planning method, evaluating what you want the outcome to be.

Dissect the process, allowing students to practice in class. One way to do this is to divide students into small groups to look at an assignment. Ask them to annotate the assignment and try to figure out the "point" of it. Once they can do this, ask them to generate a new assignment that seeks to attain the same learning outcomes as the original. Either allow for multiple iterations of the assignment or have the class determine which one of the student samples should be the basis for an actual assignment. Over time, this practice will become a part of classroom culture, as will students' expectations of participating in the development of how they extend their thinking at home and other learning experiences.

Step 2: Furnish feedback on home learning ideas.

As students work on developing new ideas for activities outside of class, it is vital that teachers and peers provide specific feedback on student proposals. Students need to know if they are headed in the right direction. If they aren't, they need to be redirected as quickly as possible. Teachers can give feedback in a number of ways: set up a system in which peer leaders in each group are responsible for feedback, meet with small groups in class so as to not create additional work outside of class, or have students submit ideas via Google Docs and provide feedback on the documents directly. You can learn more about ways to get students involved as peer reviewers in *Empower Students to Give Feedback: Teaching Students to Provide Effective Peer Feedback*, in which Starr gives detailed advice on how to construct these systems.

Step 3: Involve parents in the process.

Sometimes learning doesn't have to come from school. Parents may encounter opportunities outside of the classroom that meaningfully advance student learning. If you maintain an open line with parents, they can supplement classroom learning with family learning, like when cooking a family meal or putting together a new bookshelf. Always keep communication channels open; we'll take a closer look at teaming up with families in Hack 9. These connections may wind up being beneficial for the whole class.

Step 4: Practice saying "yes" instead of "no." Sometimes the most valuable lessons come from ideas that don't work out.

It's easy enough to say no to students if you hear something different than what you want or expect, such as when you already have an idea planned. Unfortunately, this may be a knee-jerk reaction. So it's important to pause and take in what the student is suggesting. Really listen to him/her. Ask questions about alignment with learning objectives and what the new homework will look like. It doesn't need to be an interrogation but rather clarification and follow-up questions. Sometimes it's a good idea to let students follow their own paths, even if you suspect it won't work out the way they plan. Failure serves as a wonderful learning experience in itself.

Step 5: Reflect on choices and development as a part of the process.

Reflection is key to the learning process. Although reflection may not need to be documented and/or submitted like homework, it's necessary to make it a conscious part of the metacognitive journey. We should encourage students to reflect in ways that work for them and that will provide the best returns for time spent. Some may enjoy writing publicly on a blog or privately in a journal. Some may like to talk, or Vox with themselves. Some may enjoy vlogging or just having conversations with friends about learning. Ultimately, we'd like students to develop the habit of documenting their thinking processes, but this should be organic documentation and not forced, as the latter can ruin opportunities for authentic growth. Try not to limit kids to what works for you as a teacher. Offer suggestions, but be okay if they don't take them.

Step 6: Foster sharing of ideas.

Great ideas deserve to be shared, and so does the learning that comes from them. If a student has an idea worth sharing, make time in class to allow him/her to do so. Potential sharing options include gallery walks for multiple ideas at once, thereby generating full class conversations; short presentations; or having students create multimedia experiences to recount their learning. Any time we highlight or showcase brilliant student work, we show kids that their ideas matter. Do more of this in school and don't only focus on the critical/constructive/negative feedback that often plays too much of a crucial role in students' lives.

Step 7: Celebrate student choices and adopt new ideas (always make sure to give them credit).

If what students have created is replicable, then it should be replicated. What an amazing legacy for students if one of their homework ideas ends up in the curriculum for future classes. Always ask permission from students to share their ideas and give credit when using their ideas in the future. For example, if one student develops a research project around solving a local problem as suggested in Don Wettrick's Hack in Action, why not work with that student to track the steps so other students can replicate the process to solve other problems? Once the students see the success one student has had, they will be challenged to try to solve problems that are more personally pressing for each of them.

One other example is to coordinate feature projects that incorporate students' passions. We know that when interest is high students will create their own inquiry around a topic. Ask them to find experts in the field to talk to for real-world connections rather than asking them to do research only online or in books. Once they do the research and write or develop their multimedia project, display it on the student media outlet or within the school so that more students and community members have access to the excellent learning. Having students share their hard work and even speak about it can inspire other students to do the same.

OVERCOMING PUSHBACK

Folks who favor the traditional will say that students aren't capable of coming up with comparably effective and rigorous homework ideas. They will insist that it's a teacher's job to design and determine the outcomes of learning. However, when we offer students the chance to get involved with planning how to deepen or extend their learning, their proposals often surprise even the biggest naysayers.

Students won't come up with sufficiently rigorous activities. Yes, there may be students who don't know how to seek out or express their interests, and some may compensate by taking "the easy way out." Kids are inherently curious. If we know what they like and have a decent relationship with them, it's simple to engage students in a dialogue that leads to meaningful activities.

Some students may require scaffolds, but this doesn't mean that they are incapable of generating challenging ideas for learning. Know your students and put plans in place that will best facilitate their success. Don't be afraid to have different accountability measures, such as a journal to record ideas in writing, for more challenging students. Just because there will be a required check-in doesn't make it less of their own choice, especially if we allow them to help determine the means in which they will be accountable. Once they show that they can be responsible, you can take off the training wheels.

Educators are paid to teach students how to learn. Helping students design learning activities and reflect on the impact of independent learning is more accurate. Although there will always be parents, students, and colleagues who believe that everything that happens in the classroom is the teacher's job to create, we know that the more agency we give students, the more they engage with their own learning. Einstein and others have said that it isn't the teacher's job to control the learning but rather the teacher's job to construct an environment in which optimal learning occurs. By giving students choice and voice in what and how they learn, the teacher honors each child's individual needs and embraces those differences to engender a better learning environment for all.

Kids need to know how to follow directions; they won't always have choices. We love this pushback. We hear it often, and it's important to discuss. Although there are times in our adult lives when following directions is key, knowing when to make suggestions to better the experience has always been a hallmark of the jobs we've had. We want to raise students to be innovators, capable of thinking on their own and not just mindlessly implementing instructions. How better to teach them this than to actually empower them?

THE HACK IN ACTION

Don Wettrick is the Innovation Coordinator at Noblesville High School, just outside Indianapolis, Indiana. He is the author of *Pure Genius: Building a Culture of Innovation and Taking 20% Time to the Next Level*. Wettrick has worked as a middle school and high school teacher, educational and innovation consultant, and speaker. Most important, Don works with educators, students, and entrepreneurs to bring innovation and collaborative skills into education. In this Hack in Action, Don shares how students go on research journeys of their own choosing to solve problems to better their communities.

Don's Story

I run an Innovation class at Noblesville High School, where we don't assign homework as a general rule. The class is basically a 20% time model, but instead of working on a project for 20% of the class, the class IS the students' 20% time. We felt that students needed a class period to work on things that interested them. So while we support all the foundational classes, we carved out a part of the school day to center around the student; to support what they want to learn. This could be anything, but most important it must be student-generated and focused. This is the heart of what a Genius Hour is, a time and space created specifically for the exploration of student interests and passions with the supports and resources students need to follow those curiosities.

AUTHOR COMMENT

We love framing research around a problem that matters to students. This form of inquiry is the truest form of learning and problem-solving that there is. It happens on so many levels: not just grand inquiries, but simple ones like finding alternatives to ingredients that aren't in the house. What a great way to teach students to solve everyday problems!

Two years ago a student in my innovation class, Jess Elliott, decided to embark on a journey that turned a "homework" research assignment into a two-year project. She had done some research on light pollution and saw that it was a major issue but received little attention. The research indicated that our night sky was causing various problems in nature, from birds flying into buildings to insomnia problems in humans. The biggest culprit was big cities—streetlights, neon signs, and security lighting—but what could be done about it?

In Jess's research she discovered that a lot of light pollution could be fixed by simply pointing streetlights down. Though many decorative "acorn lights" light up the sky, the energy efficient "cobra head" lenses use less energy AND light only the ground. This is where most "homework assignments" would have come to an end. There might have been an essay and poster combo, maybe even a survey, or QR code. But instead Jess decided to "think global and act local."

She reached out to local politicians, who in turn wanted her to help write a bill. This process took several months and ended up being a great learning opportunity. While I would like to say that the bill writing went well, the bill was eventually sent to a committee, where (Jess felt) it got too watered down. After seven months of ups and downs, she could have quit on this project. But Jess decided to go in another direction.

She got involved with organizations like the "International Dark Skies Association" (IDA) and started contacting members for their insights. She blogged, she networked, she persevered.

What Jess emerged with was a plan to work with land developers. She felt that enticing builders to install energy efficient street lamps would not only

> **AUTHOR COMMENT**
>
> We hear about these projects as very rare, special occurrences, but they should be more widespread. Start small with students, in attainable bites. Teach them how to find organizations that they can link up with. Show them who to reach out to and then get their parents involved to make it happen.

benefit the environment but also the financial bottom line. She is working on getting neighborhoods "Energy Star" certified for using lower wattage LED bulbs, and also for cutting down on light pollution.

When Jess wasn't working with the land developers, she was reaching out to universities for support. She gave presentations to university classes, gaining additional insights and establishing partnerships. She even decided to work with area elementary schools, where she would read a children's book about light pollution and what the students could do to help! All of this "homework" was student-directed, and she updated me based on the pacing and deadlines that we agreed upon.

Jess took TWO YEARS to work on the light pollution project, and it started with a "homework" assignment. An assignment to find out what she was passionate about. When we allot time for our students to discover a passion and ACT on it, magic happens.

And isn't that the point of education anyway? To learn about things YOU are curious about? I'm all about learning things "I ought to," but more excited about the things that have really sparked my interest.

Although Jess's two-year study may not be typical, as a great number of us don't have the chance to loop with students, Don's story shows us the power of choice and the power of Genius Hour. Giving students the opportunity to follow their own interests in a meaningful way on their own time, with all the support they need, increases their motivation and dedication to learning; learning isn't just for a grade or to comply with a policy, it's driven by self-interest. This is the purest form of learning, as it will stay with students throughout their lives.

As we continue to make out-of-school learning about kids and not about grades in books or compliance, offering students choice and voice in how they spend their own time cultivates a love for learning and develops essential life and critical thinking skills that will produce more functional adults. Merely prescribing what must be done is not learning. We must encourage students to find what they love to do and then seek it out in meaningful ways.

You just read
Hack 8: Amplify Student Voice
from

Read more at Amazon.com

HACKING
PROJECT BASED LEARNING

SHIFT THE OWNERSHIP
OF ASSESSMENT

Facilitate a Progress Assessment Tool

Students can hit any target that they know
about and that stands still for them.
— RICK STIGGINS, EDUCATOR AND AUTHOR

THE PROBLEM: ASSESSING PROJECT BASED LEARNING

A S STUDENTS ARE engaged in the controlled chaos that often characterizes PBL, teachers and administrators often have two questions regarding assessment: How will my students and I know they are learning what they are supposed to learn? How will I assess this?

Just the thought of rubrics, checklists, and scoring guidelines can be completely overwhelming. We created the Progress Assessment Tool (PAT) to facilitate self-assessment and feedback (and grading, if necessary) in the most straightforward way possible.

THE HACK: SHIFT THE OWNERSHIP OF ASSESSMENT

While the importance of grading PBL (and grades in general) can be debated, the fact remains that individual students still need to develop skills and demonstrate understanding of content, both of which should correlate with curriculum documents and/or standards. A well-crafted assessment tool (no matter who makes it) should assist with assessing these skills and understandings by making student progress visible.

> If we want the emphasis to be on the learning and not the grading, we ultimately want to give our students a tool that helps them to self- and peer-assess throughout the PBL process.

Students who shape how they are assessed own their learning because they can then make connections between their learning and the High Impact Takeaways for which they are aiming, and they know what they have to do to produce exemplary work, while maintaining enough flexibility to exercise their creativity.

The Progress Assessment Tool (PAT), shown in Table 6.1, is a three-column grid, which allows a class to collaboratively establish what exemplary work looks like for each one of the project's learning targets. Students then use the tool, with the support of their teacher, to track their progress toward these learning targets. The driving force behind the PAT is students grappling with exemplars and uncovering their strengths, which they can then use to inform their own work. By the time students are done analyzing these exemplars they are so entrenched in what quality work looks like that making it their own is significantly easier.

Progress Assessment Tool

Project Title:_____

Learning Targets	Strengths	Self-Reflection & Feedback

Table 6.1 Access a digital copy: tinyurl.com/hackingpblpat

WHAT YOU CAN DO TOMORROW

- **Prepare your Progress Assessment Tool template.** The basic format of the Progress Assessment Tool is a three-column grid.

  - **Left column** – All of your project's learning targets, each one in a separate row.

  - **Center column** – A list of student-created strengths for each target.

  - **Right column** – The right column is left intentionally blank. As students use the PAT throughout the project, this column will serve as a space for reflection and for collecting feedback from classmates and the teacher. (We discuss feedback in-depth in the next hack.)

  The PAT's value is rooted in the conversations and collaboration that take place as the class establishes the tool's content. In *A Blueprint for Full Implementation* we discuss how to populate this resource. Table 6.2 displays a completed PAT for Ross's pinball project and may provide context as you read.

- **Collect exemplars.** To better familiarize yourself with the practice of using high-quality examples to drive student work, begin collecting exemplars. These can be used for all kinds of learning, even if you are not currently engaged in a PBL unit. For example, if you are teaching informational writing by asking students to create a restaurant review, gather reviews from newspapers, Yelp, or food blogs. Alternatively, if your students will engage in solving a problem facing their local area, you may collect examples of public service announcements, fundraising websites, infographics, or flyers. The key here is variety. We want to expose students to multiple options so their creativity is not limited.

- **Analyze exemplars.** For a current or future unit, which may or may not be PBL, have students analyze exemplars and ask them to infuse their quality characteristics into their work. For example, if students are going to be creating advertisements, they can examine advertisements from across different channels: television commercials, radio ads, magazine ads, etc. While doing so they can create a list of effective characteristics all these mediums have in common and then use these characteristics to help drive what they do.

- **Empower your students to be critical evaluators.** Many of your students are probably not familiar with how to critically evaluate their own work, and almost every educator knows students who will complete a task and submit without so much as a second glance. Invite your students to use your current rubric, checklist, or grading guidelines to assess their own work. Challenge the class to identify specific areas in need of improvement, and collaborate with students, in small groups or individually, to develop action steps for moving forward.

A BLUEPRINT FOR FULL IMPLEMENTATION

Step 1: Determine what learning targets to assess (left column).

In Hack 3, you established your High Impact Content. Your students need to demonstrate understanding of this content in order to master the High Impact Takeaways for the project. Therefore, your PAT will include all of the learning targets that make up your HIC.

115

Progress Assessment Tool

Project Title: **Pinball wizard**

Learning Targets	Strengths	Self-Reflection & Feedback
Explain how an object's change in motion can be observed and measured.	• Clear examples/explanations of how Newton's Laws of Motion relate to each group's specific pinball machine	
Apply knowledge of basic electrical circuits to the design and construction of simple direct current circuits.	• The circuit contains a closed path, which connects a light bulb to a battery • The circuit contains a switch, which can be activated by a pinball	
Understand that systems have parts and components that work together.	• Clear explanations of why a pinball machine qualifies as a system, including scientific vocabulary: interdependent, boundaries, structure and purpose, etc.	
Describe the engineering process.	• Thoughtful planning of project design • Clear explanations of why project iterations were necessary	
Recognize and use everyday symbols to communicate key ideas.	• Blueprint symbols (e.g., measurements, angles, electrical components) clearly communicate plans	
Identify and use simple hand tools correctly and safely.	• The right tool is appropriately used for the right job • No one is hurt while using tools • Tools are cared for, for the benefit of all students and groups	

Table 6.2

In Hack 3 you also established your supporting content. Your supporting content is more of a judgment call when deciding what learning targets to include. If the content is going to be taught and assessed within the context of your HIC, there is no reason to list it separately on your PAT. However, when it comes to vocabulary and facts, you can consider assessing it through other means, such as a quiz during the project to make sure students learn the necessary basics leading up to their HITs.

If a statement contains only one student action, you can also consider this statement a learning target and it can go straight into your PAT. However, if a statement calls for multiple actions, it may be necessary to break it down into multiple learning targets (which can then be inserted into your PAT).

A Grade 8 English Language Arts standard reads: "Introduce claims, acknowledge and distinguish the claims from alternate or opposing claims, and organize the reasons and evidence logically." We can turn this standard into learning targets by simplifying the statement into its specific parts:

- Introduce claims

- Acknowledge and distinguish the claims from alternate or opposing claims

- Organize the reasons and evidence logically

The extent to which the standard is broken down depends on the degree to which the individual skills are dependent upon each other. For example, it would be possible for students to be able to introduce a claim without appropriately acknowledging alternate claims. Therefore, both of these skills should be listed separately. Finally, prior to using any learning target, we highly recommend rewording it in student-friendly language, if needed.

Step 2: Extract strengths from exemplars.

After your learning targets have been established, students will need a clear idea of what it looks like to meet each one. To provide this clarity, students, in groups of about four to five, will analyze exemplars to create a list of strengths (think: bullet points) for each learning target.

Give each group your list of learning targets and exemplars containing strengths that embody the type of work you would ideally see from your students. After reviewing the learning targets, groups analyze the exemplars with the targets in mind. For each target, they generate a list of strengths that demonstrate its mastery.

Encourage students to focus on strengths that are as specific as possible and don't necessarily rely on the medium in which they exist. The goal is for students to uncover that the same strengths can be exhibited in several ways. To drive this point home, it is important for groups to review exemplars from across different mediums. For example, for a PBL unit on opinions/arguments, groups examined sample essays and TED Talks. One of the strengths found was, "Evidence to support claims from life experience." Notice how this strength can exist practically anywhere, as it is not tied to a specific method of delivery (yet, no matter the method of delivery, the same learning target could be satisfied).

For other projects, it may be necessary to look at portions of the project separately. For example, the pinball machines created by Ross's students had to contain a working simple circuit. Rather than observing a pinball machine as a whole, they focused on this one element to establish success criteria. In this instance, the success criterion was something to the effect of "The circuit contains a closed path, which connects a light bulb to a battery." Notice how this statement is specific but still open-ended enough for students to be able to determine many of the details regarding their own circuits.

Step 3: Crowdsource strengths (center column).

All of the students come together, and each group brings along the strengths they found in the exemplars. The purpose of this large group session is to sort through these strengths to develop a definitive list of strengths for each learning target. For each target, create a separate class list on chart paper, on a whiteboard, or in your favorite polling software. Include the relevant strengths from each group's list (what relates to the learning target) and make sure to exclude possible duplicates. After the lists have been curated, conduct a class discussion to ensure only the most relevant strengths are included. Place your final list of strengths adjacent to its learning target in column two of the PAT.

Step 4: Revising, Editing, and Publishing.

As the facilitator, it will be essential for you to take a critical look at the PAT to ensure there are no gaps, and there is a direct correlation between satisfying a learning target and its list of strengths. In other words, a student has demonstrated mastery of a target if she has satisfied its list of strengths. If any significant changes are going to be made, consult with your students, as you do not want them to lose ownership and feel like their work was not taken seriously. Once the work is refined, it can be distributed to students. Also, you can consider creating and distributing a digital version through Google Drive or another cloud storage system. This format will give you and your students whenever, wherever access, which will be valuable as feedback is provided throughout the project.

OVERCOMING PUSHBACK

Standard, teacher-made rubrics have the tendency to overwhelm learners and interfere with student agency, as they are overly prescriptive and often focus on task completion rather than learning outcomes. Creating more opportunities for students to be intimately involved in the assessment process will ensure greater transfer of learning between tasks.

All of this work with exemplars takes too much time. After a project is launched, students are often excited as they actively toss around ideas. Once they begin working, they become so entrenched in these ideas that they often forget to look at their work with a critical eye. Taking the time to explore exemplars and establish high-quality strengths will assist students in fine-tuning their process and their product.

Doesn't this kill inquiry? Give special consideration as to when learning targets are revealed to students, as providing the information too early may be tantamount to a comedian supplying the punchline to a joke before starting the joke itself. In other words, there may be much more value in students uncovering the targets (and then being "formally" told what they are by the teacher), as opposed to the teacher simply providing a list of everything that is to be learned for the upcoming unit. Selecting when to create your PAT is dependent on the length of your project, so pinning down an exact day is not entirely formulaic. However, you may want to start working on the PAT with your students after they have had time to explore and inquire (after the project launch), but before they are too far into creating a final product.

This wouldn't work with the students I have. If necessary, the PAT creation steps we detail could be adapted to meet the needs of your students. For example, if you are working with younger students, the entire process of extracting strengths from exemplars could be done as a whole class. Meanwhile, if you are working with older students, they could use the exemplars to uncover strengths *and* the learning targets for which they are aiming.

Rubrics are better. If we want the emphasis to be on the learning and not the grading, we ultimately want to give our students a tool that helps them to self- and peer-assess throughout the PBL process. While traditional rubrics can be valuable, all of the 4s, 3s, 2s, and 1s can be overwhelming, even for adults. Meanwhile, it is generally easier for students to make use of a PAT due to its less-is-more approach, and it still includes what really matters in learning targets, strengths pertaining to each target (which could be categorized as 4s), and feedback. For grading purposes, if teachers feel a rubric is necessary, they could easily convert any PAT into a rubric by incorporating the 3s, 2s, and 1s after the fact.

THE HACK IN ACTION

Jen Brinson is a high school social studies and gifted support teacher who has over twenty years' experience with student-created assessments. Here she details how her students have designed their own Progress Assessment Tools.

> Toward the beginning of my career in my Advanced Placement U.S. History class, I assigned a project on the Civil War. The students were able to choose their topics and their mediums for presentation, which were largely limited to the non-digital variety. Upon assigning the project, I asked the class what I should look for as I assessed their work. We constructed a list of qualities and learning criteria, and when students were finished with their contributions I inquired, "If these are the requirements for an average project, what does an A look like?" Average, you see, is a C. I was looking for exceptional. After much groaning, we buckled down and got to work, further defining the criteria for an exceptional project.
>
> The lesson learned from this exercise was that students must have ownership of their work and how it is to be assessed. They know what they deem to be important, and they should be able to articulate what they value. As educators, it is critical we listen carefully to our students' views. Sometimes, what we value isn't consistent with what is valued by our students. This isn't to say we compromise our standards, but we must be in tune with how our students are interpreting the worth of what they are learning.

To guide the conversation for student-created assessments, a couple of questions are important: What is important to know (content)? How will you demonstrate your learning? Conversations can self-propel at this point, as students generally have a lot to say when responding to these questions.

In our discussions of the French Revolution, students have two projects to complete: an Autopsy of a Revolution (Umbrella Question: What is a revolution?) and a project on the major personalities of the French Revolution (Umbrella Question: What is a legacy?). Students have many opportunities to choose their presentation mediums and the knowledge they wish to include. With those choices they also have plenty of ideas as to what should be assessed and how much value to assign to each criteria. This assessment creation conversation cannot occur until some time has been spent on initial research and product creation, as students are not initially aware of what aspects of their work should carry more value.

Once the class is ready to engage in the assessment creation process, we begin by discussing what the average project entails. Then, we ramp up the criteria so it is suitable for an exceptional project, and we pare it down for a "not yet successful" project. The conversation flows due to the two initial questions—What is important to know? How will you demonstrate your learning? Other questions an instructor may need to use to prompt input could include: What are the standards? What is the role of creativity? What is the role of critical thinking? What is the role of collaboration? What is the role of communication? What is the role of clarity in your work?

Progress Assessment Tools are an effective way to not only drive conversations about what students value, but to also inspire reflection and deeper planning. I always encourage my students to not only self-assess their work, but to pass it off to a peer to evaluate how they would assess their work according to the final PAT. This self- and peer-evaluation process allows students the opportunity to reflect and refine their work and, ultimately, their learning.

Regarding PBL, teachers often ask, "How will my students and I know they are learning what they are supposed to learn?" and "How will I assess this?" A Progress Assessment Tool answers both of these questions.

A PAT helps students to first understand what is expected of them, and then leverage these expectations to drive their own work while being able to constantly self- and/or peer-assess and adjust their process accordingly. Feedback is another critical component of this assessment process, which we will discuss in the next hack.

You just read
Hack 6: Shift The Ownership Of Assessment
from

Read more at Amazon.com

VIGOR VERSUS RIGOR

Meet the challenge without becoming paralyzed

*More options, even good ones, can freeze us
and make us retreat to the default plan.*
—CHIP HEATH, AUTHOR

THE PROBLEM: IT'S NOT AS RIGOROUS AS YOU THINK

RIGOR HAS BEEN one of the buzziest educational words since the advent of the Common Core. Vendors have honed in on rigor as a selling point, highlighting the term to market their wares. The bigger the company, the more intense the rigor, or at least that's what they'd have you believe. There's big money in being the most rigorous version of Common Core aligned materials available. The real problem is these products aren't necessarily as rigorous as they think they are.

There's a big difference between more work and better work. Vendors, who don't know your population of kids personally, should never be the ones directing traffic in your classroom. Perhaps it would be beneficial to closely read the documents associated with your vendor product.

Does it rely heavily on a particular strategy or type of formative assessment, such as close reading each page of a story or using exit tickets at the end of every lesson? Does it include more practice with mathemat-ical problems or more comprehension ques-tions than there were in previous iterations of the resource? Do its prescriptive steps negate the need for you to have a teaching degree to deliver the material? Are the materials geared toward a generalized audience of students?

Vigor is the word you're really looking for.

That's not rigor. That's just more stuff with a side of distrust in your abili-ties. Common sense and Common Core aren't mutually exclusive.

THE HACK: GO DEEP WITH VIGOR INSTEAD

This is a one-letter hack. Change the first "r" in rigor to a "v." Vigor is the word you're really looking for. I know it's just semantics, but sometimes changing little things has a big impact. We're seeking opportunities for depth. We're seeking authentic growth with engagement. I don't think depth, authentic growth, or engagement will happen when we focus so intently on rigor, a word that connotes strictness, severity, and stiffness.

Vigor, conversely, connotes robustness, health, strength, and har-diness. It makes me think of dynamic and enthusiastic learning, of interactive and innovative learning environments, and of organic and authentic learning moments. All things I associate with depth. Vigor is a word that makes me think of the joy in learning—perhaps the joy *of* learning. I've written much over the years about engagement in the learning process. You can't have real learning if you don't have real engagement. Students need an emotional anchor. They need something to connect to that they aren't likely to forget. Vigorous learning experi-ences provide anchors for real learning.

This means that we need to consider how vigorous our curriculum is in light of the Common Core Standards. Skills are important, but equally so are imagination, creativity, and inquiry. They should never be separated.

WHAT **YOU** CAN DO TOMORROW

1. **Appraise your current week's curriculum.** Take out this week's plan and look for items that are invigorating and items that are the monotonous same-old, same-old. Replace anything boring with something more exciting. For instance, if math practice consists of a worksheet or an often-used strategy, switch it up with some manipulatives. Call out a number and have students use the manipulatives to create visual equations as quickly as possible. Use pennies, buttons, checkers, or anything you've got. Perhaps your students are drawing angles or shapes. What about a field trip around the school to take pictures of the angles or shapes you're studying? Come back to the classroom and organize the pictures. Use rulers and protractors to measure the images and compare what you collected. Perhaps students are taking a spelling or vocabulary test. Have them use the words to tell a story orally first, then ask them to write down as much of the story as they can remember, maybe using a digital tool like Storybird or Google Docs. Be sure to add visuals for maximum engagement.

2. **Share your intentions.** Let your colleagues or teammates know what you're thinking and look for opportunities to share vigorous practices. Talk regularly with your grade level or content area team about your engagement strategies for the coming

week. Share your plans and create opportunities to brainstorm about each other's work.

3. Practice engagement habits. Engagement habits will help you to work fun into your curriculum. Get into the habit of asking yourself two questions: 1) How often am I creating engaging opportunities for my students? and 2) In what ways am I creating engaging opportunities for my students? Easy and effective answers to these two questions involve offering choices to students. Those choices could include differentiated products, processes, media, technology tools, or even choices in assessments.

4. Ask the students. In the 21st century, student voice and input is essential to buy-in and real learning more than ever. Provide your students with opportunities to make decisions about how they will learn and demonstrate their learning. Note how those choices positively affect their learning and determine which types of choices help students to do their best work. Students need to know that their voices are being heard and valued. Students need to know that their opinions matter and that they have choices in the way that they learn something and the way that they will be assessed.

A BLUEPRINT FOR FULL IMPLEMENTATION

Step 1: Appraise your curriculum.

Systematically look at your yearlong curriculum. Start with the current unit and work your way forward. If you're reading this mid-year, it's fine to wait until the summer to revise the units you've already completed. Look for opportunities to inject joy, creativity, awe, technology, PBL, STEAM, engagement, and personalization. Vigor is like seasoning. Put it in every recipe! To beef up the zest and robustness of your curriculum, makes sure the verbs in your unit plans match the verbs in the standards. Adjust verbs in assessments so they match as well. Appraise your curriculum for thinking. Vigorous units, while being engaging, should also scaffold thinking. Certainly, students should be able to recognize and identify content pieces, but they need many opportunities to apply, evaluate, and create too. All levels of thinking should be in a vigorous curriculum.

Step 2: Create a culture of shared curriculum design.

Converse, collaborate, and come to consensus with all stakeholders. Sometimes you can discover meaningful ways to engage, teach, or assess by asking your colleagues and your students. Document these conversations in your curriculum units and remind everyone in the design process how valuable their input is. Share goals and objectives with students ahead of time and ask them about their vision for demonstrating how they might get there. Add their ideas to the plan or let them create a menu of options that would allow them some choice in activities and assessments.

Step 3: Make learning fun again.

Let's get back to what really matters in learning. Vigorous learning makes acquisition and application of knowledge so memorable that teachers can simultaneously engage enduring understandings and work above the curriculum, virtually guaranteeing that students will never forget what they've learned/participated in/created. Vigorous learning spans differentiations, includes everyone's unique contributions, and gives kids the voices they need. If they are participators (through action, design, conversation, etc.), then they are learners.

Let me say that again: *If the kids are participators, they are learners.* Purposeful design and purposeful practice prompt so many implications for learning and making that learning stick.

Step 4: Introduce PBL and STEM/STEAM.

In problem based learning (PBL), students seek to solve an authentic problem using research skills and critical thinking while building content knowledge. STEM and STEAM have to do with engineering tasks, creating a product using related science, technology, math, and arts skills.

> **Learning shouldn't be the soupe du jour; it should be a buffet.**

In some schools, the emphasis is on the science or the technology or the mathematics, but in my experience, engineering the product should be the focal point, with the other content areas orbiting it. Having PBL or STEM/STEAM projects in your curriculum open up multiple options for students to research and study authentic projects and issues, building opportunities for engagement and deep learning. Real engagement is where joy and awe live in the curriculum.

OVERCOMING PUSHBACK

We don't have time for fun. There's a scene in the movie *Hocus Pocus* when the witches in the story come across a school in Salem, Massachusetts. The other witches ask what this building is and Bette Midler's character, Winifred, takes a look at the drab exterior, the peeling paint, the wrought iron and pointy fence, and determines that it is a prison for children. When teachers tell me that they don't have time for fun or joy or awe or depth, this is what I think of. If teachers aren't providing experiences their students will remember, keeping everything "the way we've always done it," school certainly does sound like prison to me—imagine how the kids feel. What teachers are really saying when they say they don't have time for fun is that they don't have time for learning. It's never a surprise to me when baffled teachers tell me that they covered their curriculum and they did loads of test prep, but the kids still didn't perform. Why should they? Teachers didn't give them incentives to learn; they only provided students with opportunities to receive knowledge the way they receive candy from a Pez dispenser. That's not teaching or learning, and there's nothing in that method that makes the learning stick. If you really care about learning and performance, then you have to care about fun and engagement. They go hand-in-hand, like Forrest Gump and Jenny or peas and carrots.

The administrator wants vigor but also wants me to use a vendor product with a high degree of fidelity. As with other similar issues, the answer is that the team needs to talk. Conversation, collaboration, and consensus are really important here. You must talk about what's worth keeping and what needs to be deleted from your vendor products. If we want vigorous instruction and engagement, fun, and joy, then we have to think of our specific population of kids as a lens through which we look at the curriculum. We can't apply a generalized curriculum to a specific group of children in the same way we can't give aspirin to every malady and have it work. Curriculum needs to be targeted and focused like a laser for each specific population of students. If you must adhere to a vendor product, then you must evaluate its many facets. Use only the components and resources that benefit your students—chuck everything else. Then find ways to inject your class with joy and authenticity.

Our population of students is working nowhere near grade level, so how can I do more vigorous work with them? Vigor isn't necessarily in what is on grade level; rather, it is in what challenges the individual student. This means that teachers have to pay attention to their students' interests, their abilities, and their performances.

Teachers must analyze whether faulty performance is due to an interest issue or a learning issue. If it's lack of interest, then talk to the student and see if there is some alternate way for the student to demonstrate proficiency. If it's a gap in learning, scaffold instruction so that the student has a more manageable way to attain the goal. Offer more choices in the ways students learn and the ways they can demonstrate their learning. Learning shouldn't be the soupe du jour; it should be a buffet. Choices matter here, and the more choices a student has in learning and in assessment, the more accurately you can determine whether that student actually gets it. Students who have choices and are engaged will likely level up faster and attain grade-level expectations if they are supported appropriately.

THE HACK IN ACTION

In a city middle school in downtown Manhattan, teachers were frustrated with students' performance on the New York State Common Core Assessments. During professional development, teachers discussed how the scores were a "checkup," like taking a person's pulse at one moment in time, and they weren't meant to diagnose students' learning needs. However, the test scores had been low for two years in a row and they agreed that they needed to improve their approach.

This school had been using curriculum materials supplied to New York State by vendors who had won state contracts. There was a vendor for English language arts and a separate vendor for mathematics. Their administrator had tasked teachers with following the materials with fidelity, but clearly that level of adherence to the program was not getting them the results they wanted. While they didn't want to put all of their eggs in the state test basket, they were concerned that students were also underperforming on their benchmark assessments throughout the year despite the fact that teachers were steadfastly staying on track with their vendor-supplied curriculum.

I worked with these teachers to appraise their curriculum for contemporary practices. The teachers discovered that the vendor product was generalized for a large population. It didn't address what they believed were necessities, primarily regarding technology, choices in the learning process, and varied methods for formative and summative assessments.

We decided it would be beneficial to brainstorm opportunities to replace the generalized practices and assessments of the vendor products with more contemporary methods that truly represented their specific student population.

In particular, they looked at the products' assessments and instructional methodologies with an eye to integrating lively and contemporary revisions. They brainstormed ways to inject choice, fun, and authenticity into their instructional practices and brainstormed alternatives to the suggested assessments.

They also looked for opportunities for overlap in their professional practices and places to integrate content areas such as science and social studies into the language arts classes. They looked specifically at individual lesson plans and sought to replace rote activities with opportunities to explore and discover rather than "sit and get."

This school had begun mapping its curriculum even before the Common Core Standards had come into play. Teachers used existing curriculum mapping software to document the changes to the vendor's curriculum so that content area and grade-level decisions were visible to the whole organization.

Documenting their curriculum also conveniently pinpointed future professional development opportunities to address gaps and overlaps in the standards and to discuss their practical application. As of this publication, the school has yet to receive its current year's test scores, but the teachers feel confident that performance improved significantly because students were more engaged and had a more cerebral experience than in previous years. Students also performed better on benchmark assessments than they had since implementation of the Common Core Standards.

Many of the teachers commented on their improved morale when they heard students "oohing and aahing" over instructional activities that they had updated based on their collaborative conversations. After many years of feeling beaten down, they were finally starting to feel like they were making a difference again. There's no better feeling in the world for an educator.

Vigor doesn't mean heaping on more work. It means finding ways to engage students in opportunities for deep, rich learning. "The way we've always done it" won't work anymore, and neither will putting a fresh coat of paint on a traditional practice. We have to re-imagine contemporary teaching and learning, integrating vigor into instruction.

You just read
Hack 7: Vigor Versus Rigor
from

Read more at Amazon.com

CONCLUSION

GOOD LUCK

BLEAK NEWS GREETED me in the summer of 2010. I was five years from retirement. While I had always enjoyed teaching, part of me was ready to commence a new chapter in my life. Thirty years is a long time to do anything. But thirty years doesn't come close to representing the average American life span. I've never permitted my job to define me, so I was looking forward to spending the next five years planning my next professional excursion.

On our teacher workday that fateful August, the day before the students arrived, I learned that the State of Ohio's Public Employee Retirement Systems had been devastated by the Recession of 2008. The upshot was my October 2015 retirement target would be undermined. I'm a positive person, but it was like being informed in the last few miles of a marathon that the race would be extended.

> It suddenly dawned on me how selfish I'd been. I remembered what an awesome privilege it is to help kids blossom.

The next twenty-four hours were painful. I felt like I'd fulfilled my part of the obligation to the good people of Ohio. I like having a plan, and this development really shook me. As has happened frequently in my career when I've been confronted by significant personal challenges, all those feelings of turmoil evaporated at 7:30 a.m. the next day—the first day of school. A sweet fourteen-year-old girl marched up to me, smiled, and raised her right hand. I looked at her quizzically, but then I instinctively raised my right hand too. Then I caught on and we high-fived one another. She said, "I'm so glad you're my teacher. I've heard awesome things about you."

I thanked her and then quickly shuffled down the hall to the small men's room in the faculty lounge. I shut the door, locked it, rotated to a corner, and broke into passionate sobs. It was so intense, so unexpected. It suddenly dawned on me how selfish I'd been. I remembered what an awesome privilege it is to help kids blossom.

I composed myself, blew my nose, stared at myself in the mirror, and thought *If you're going to be a teacher for the foreseeable future, be a great one.*

In August of 2016 I'll begin my thirty-second year of bonding, encouraging, and learning from youngsters. And there's no end in sight. I'm grateful for my experience in 2010. It shamed and inspired me. Since then, I've become a much better teacher. I'm the old guy in the building who's not afraid to try things. I've recommitted myself to compassionate teaching. I love learning new tactics from younger tech-savvy colleagues. As a result, my students have thrived.

The past five years in the classroom have been magical. I published my first book. I've made amazing friends with podcasts and on Voxer. And now, I'm so excited to offer this book, which wouldn't have been possible if it weren't for a sweet and tender compliment offered by a child on a late summer morning. Maybe I can be that motivating force for you.

This book is stocked with ideas that can transform your class. If you had the commitment and fortitude to purchase and then read these pages, your heart is in exactly the right place. This disposition is the most important part. The rest is just trial and error. Take the hacks in this book and give them a shot. Who knows? The next five years could be magical for you.

Good luck with engaging your students.

THE AUTHORS

 **Mark Barnes** is the publisher at Times 10 Books, creator of the Hack Learning Series, and host of the Hack Learning podcast. A longtime educator, Mark is the co-author of *Hacking Education* and eight other books, including the award-winning *Role Reversal*. One of the world's top connected educators, Mark's social media shares reach millions of newsfeeds monthly. Connect with him on Twitter @ markbarnes19.

 **Joe Sanfelippo** is the co-author of *Hacking Leadership*, the fifth book in the Hack Learning Series. He is the superintendent of the Fall Creek School District in Wisconsin, a U.S. Department of Education Future Ready Superintendent, and two-time Bammy Award Finalist for Superintendent of the Year. Joe has attended a Leadership Summit at the White House and is a renowned presenter. Connect with him on Twitter @joesanfelippoFC.

 **Tony Sinanis**, the co-author of *Hacking Leadership*, is the assistant superintendent at Plainedge UFSD and former lead learner at Cantiague Elementary, a National Blue Ribbon School. Tony is the 2014 New York State Elementary Principal of the Year and the 2013 Bammy Awards' National Elementary School Principal of the Year. Connect with him on Twitter @tonysinanis.

Starr Sackstein is the author of eight books, including *Hacking Assessment*, Book 3 in the Hack Learning Series. She is also the co-author of *Hacking Homework*. One of progressive education's biggest voices, Starr produces *EdWeek's* popular Work in Progress blog and co-moderates the always-trending #sunchat on Twitter. Starr is a 2014 Bammy Awards finalist for Secondary High School Educator. Connect with her on Twitter @mssackstein.

Jennifer Gonzalez is the co-author of *Hacking Education*, the first book in the Hack Learning Series. She is the publisher of the popular education site Cult of Pedagogy and author of the *Teachers Guide to Tech*. Jennifer's Cult of Pedagogy podcast is often ranked in the Top 10 on iTunes. Connect with her on Twitter @cultofpedagogy.

Angela Stockman is the author of *Make Writing*, Book 2 in the Hack Learning Series, and former lead blogger at Brilliant or Insane, where she acquired nearly one million readers in a single year. As a former English teacher and founder of the WNY Young Writer's Studio, a community of writers in Buffalo, New York, Angela brings a unique combination of experience and expertise to Hack Learning. Connect with her on Twitter at @angelastockman.

James Sturtevant followed his first book *You've Gotta Connect* with *Hacking Engagement,* Book 7 in the Hack Learning Series, making him one of education's leading experts on student engagement and rapport building. His work has been featured in the Huffington Post, Edutopia, Principal Leadership, Ohio Schools Magazine, Talks With Teachers, Join Up Dots, and many other education resources, and his Hacking Engagement podcast is one of few that features students as guests. Connect with him on Twitter @JamesSturtevant.

Gerard Dawson is the author of the *Hacking Literacy*, Book 6 in the Hack Learning Series. He teaches English and Journalism to students in grades 9-12 at Hightstown High School in New Jersey. Gerard is a contributing author to the Talks With Teachers publication, *The Best Lesson Series: Literature,* and his work has appeared in The New York Times Learning Network, Edutopia, and Brilliant or Insane, among others. Connect with him on Twitter @gerarddawson3.

Connie Hamilton is the co-author of the *Hacking Homework*, the eighth book in the Hack Learning Series. She is a K-12 curriculum director and education consultant. Connie is passionate (and a little geeky) about professional learning, particularly in the area of instructional practices such as questioning and student engagement. Connect with her on Twitter @conniehamilton.

Ross Cooper is the co-author of *Hacking Project Based Learning*, Hack Learning Series Book 9. Ross is the Supervisor of K-12 Instructional Practice in the Salisbury Township School District in Allentown, Pennsylvania. He is an Apple Distinguished Educator and a Google Certified Teacher. Connect with him on Twitter @rosscoops31

Erin Murphy is the co-author of *Hacking Project Based Learning*. She is the assistant principal at Eyer Middle School in the East Penn School District, a certified literacy specialist, and coordinator of the middle level ELA department. She has presented at numerous conferences focused on project-based learning, literacy, technology, and educational leadership. Connect with Erin on Twitter @murhpysmusings5.

Michael Fisher is the author of *Hacking the Common Core*, Book 4 in the Hack Learning Series, and eight other books. He works with schools around the country, helping to sustain curriculum upgrades, design curriculum, and modernize instruction in immersive technology. Connect with Michael on Twitter @fisher1000

HACK LEARNING RESOURCES

All Things Hack Learning:

hacklearning.org

The Entire Hack Learning Series on Amazon:

hacklearningbooks.com

The Hack Learning Podcast, hosted by Mark Barnes:

hacklearningpodcast.com

Hack Learning on Twitter:

@HackMyLearning

#HackLearning

#HackingEngagement

#HackingHomework

#HackingLeadership

#HackingLiteracy

#HackingPBL

#MakeWriting

The Hack Learning Academy:

hacklearningacademy.com

Hack Learning on Facebook:

facebook.com/hacklearningseries

The Hack Learning Store:

hacklearningstore.com

PUBLICATIONS

Times 10 is helping all education stakeholders improve every aspect of teaching and learning. We are committed to solving big problems with simple ideas. We bring you content from experts, shared through multiple channels, including books, podcasts, and an array of social networks. Our mantra is simple: Read it today; fix it tomorrow.

Stay in touch with us at #HackLearning on Twitter and on the Hack Learning Facebook page. To work with our authors and consultants, visit our Team page at hacklearning.org.

60800320R00083

Made in the USA
Lexington, KY
18 February 2017